Prayers *of* Power

Breaking Through to Wholeness

MARTIN FRANKENA

Requests for information should be addressed to:

Martin Frankena, Rushing Streams Ministries

www.rushingstreamsministries.org

Cover design and book formatting by Jon Hamill

Other books published by the Author

Becoming Light in a Dark World

ABOUT PRAYERS OF POWER

When Jesus prayed things happened; there was never any doubt. His words were true, His voice was heard, His heart was the Father's heart, His prayers were PRAYERS OF POWER.

When we pray, we must pray with the heart of Jesus, fully trusting God for the outcome. James declares that there is a prayer that is powerful, and that is the prayer of a righteous man.

May all our prayers be prayers of power— prayers that move mountains out of our lives and the lives of others.

> *I need this book! So many Christians wonder why they struggle with life. I am asked, "Why am I not getting better?" "Why is life so difficult?" As you read this book by Martin Frankena you will gain insights that will help you answer these questions!*
> —Paul L. Cox, Founder
> Aslan's Place Ministries

> *If you merely want relief from your problems, this is not the book for you. But if you want the wholeness that comes from absolute surrender to Jesus Christ, then read carefully and pray each prayer honestly. Your life can change!*
> —Kevin Miller, Vice President
> Christianity Today International

Table of Contents

Acknowledgements

I never cease to be amazed for God's wonderful provision. He called us into ministry and opened every door in the process of bringing us to a place of greater and greater wholeness, His faithfulness is beyond description and most often beyond my understanding. He keeps blessing and lifting us up to higher and higher revelation and intimacy. We delight in His constant prodding as he challenges us to move from one level of trust to the next, revealing himself in the myriad of ways that fascinate us and inspire us to keep going.

We are constantly exploring and receiving deeper revelation of His goodness, and the enemy's determination to undermine the work of God in our personal lives.

> We are constantly exploring and receiving deeper revelation of God's goodness...

When we received prophetic words to write, it seemed an impossible task; there was not enough time, or even the means or the skills needed to undertake such a project. However, the words we received from different sources where clear. Write.

It began almost imperceptibly, through the preparation of course materials, the writing of school manuals and finally the leap into book form.

In the process God opened doors that provided us with places to work and the people to help hammer thoughts into shape and form that hopefully is readable and helpful.

One of these wonderful people whom God provided is a dear friend, Carol Miller. She helped guide me through the finer aspects of grammar, nudged me to clarify and then to expand the ideas and contents.

Without her selfless help we would not have left the starting block. I owe much to her ability to question and prod me on to the next page and then the next revision. In the process we argued a lot, learned a lot and also laughed a lot.

I also want to thank Sandy Landry, who with her husband Glenn opened their home to us to finish the manuscript. Sandy took the work to the next level, further clarifying and arranging the content to give it the flow it needed. Her ability to see the structure and bring order into the flow has deeply blessed me.

Sue and Roger Ekenberg took the project to the next level by offering to have the book published. Their wonderful encouragement and faith in the project was a great motivation to bring the book to completion.

I am grateful for their generosity and kindness.

Most of all I am blessed and delighted to have my wife, Cindy, alongside to encourage and encourage and then encourage me again. Without her support the book would never have been finished.

She is God's most special gift to me.

This work is a result of exposure to so many others who have preceded us in the ministry of healing. In the thirty plus years that we have been involved in ministry we have been exposed to some of the most caring and giving individuals. They were the pioneers who broke the ground so that others might build. We look forward with great expectation to see the new generation develop further insights and new revelations for healing in the days to come.

PREFACE

In life we are faced with a myriad of problems that seem to create obstructions to the life we hoped for, whether in our relationships, jobs, finances, living circumstances or our health. Any of these can create a certain level of discomfort for us and for those around us. For the most part we can deal with the many daily inconveniences that are a part of everyday life; we can even learn to handle and live with those things that are very inconvenient or difficult for us.

However, when many of us, who are Christians, bring an issue in our lives to God, we believe and expect that He is now somehow obligated to fix the problem.

When we have prayed, fasted, read more scriptures than we can remember and still are not healed, delivered or changed, we may begin to question God's intention or commitment towards us.

One of the most frequent and difficult questions we hear about God is, "Why did he not heal... protect... save... confirm... tell me... stop... etc." From our human perspective the question does not seem to be out of place.

However, the questions we ask of God can very much be a part of the problem. *Our questions about God's commitment to our wellbeing reveal our heart towards him* and the depth of our relationship with the Father, particularly when we begin to look at our motive and the attitude behind the questions

When we question or doubt the very goodness of God's heart toward us and others, we will automatically build a wall of separation and even anger between us.

Anytime we are angry or rage at God it is misguided anger and rage; it will create even greater and therefore a greater vulnerability in our lives to the work of the enemy. We can rage at the enemy who deceived us, we can point at the sinful behavior of our forefathers, we can hate our fallen nature—but we can never blame God. *Raging at God has never changed a situation; all it does is create a greater separation from the only one who can truly help us.*

His word says that he will never leave us or forsake us:

> *Make sure that your character is free from the love of money, being content with what you have; for He Himself has said, "I WILL NEVER DESERT YOU, NOR WILL I EVER FORSAKE YOU,"* **Hebrews 13:5**

Yet, there is in us the constant questioning about these words, *"...if this is true, then why did...?"* and we can fill the blanks on almost a daily basis. His word is true, and from His perspective it is the best solution to our problem.

In the gospel of Matthew, the last word the Lord speaks to his disciples is:

"All authority has been given to Me in heaven and on earth. Go therefore and make disciples of all the nations, baptizing them in the name of the Father and the Son and the Holy Spirit, teaching them to observe all that I commanded you; and lo, I am with you always, even to the end of the age." **Matthew 28:18-20**

And again we feel that this word may apply to others, but for us this often does not seem to be the case. We call out, *"God, where are you???"* as we go through life feeling alone and forsaken.

In our frustration we judge God to be unjust and uncaring. With our limited vision, we struggle to understand that which we cannot. We turn away in anger because something has not gone the way we expected or wanted it to go. When we expect God to deal with us according to our expectation, we are attempting to lower God to our level of understanding.

"For My thoughts are not your thoughts, Nor are your ways My ways," declares the LORD. "For as the heavens are higher than the earth, So are My ways higher than your ways And My thoughts than your thoughts." **Isaiah 55:8-9**

We assume that we know all there is to know about our situation, our hearts, our future destiny and the very nature of God. Therefore, we presume that we have a right to tell him what to do and how to do it.

When we don't "get our way" with God, we become discouraged, angry or even resentful at the one who is our only hope. When Job is determined to confront God, he is really not given any satisfaction, but he is challenged in his attitude towards God.

The Message puts it this way:

> *"Do you presume to tell me what I'm doing wrong? Are you calling me a sinner so you can be a saint?* **Job 40:8** *MSG*

We cannot address the issue of why God does or doesn't do something. But we can address areas in our own lives where we have inherited or even created our own obstacles that can stop healing and freedom from flowing through our lives.

If we are not experiencing healing in our life we may have to consider the possibility that there are hindrances that are blocking or limiting the flow of healing.

> Christianity is always a personal choice.

In whatever way we address these obstacles, whether on our own or with the help of friends or prayer ministers, we need to do so with a heart willing to trust that God is for us, no matter what the outcome. God is aware of our need whether we are praying for spiritual, emotional, volitional, mental or physical healing.

INTRODUCTION

There are many reasons people are not healed. In this book we will examine some of them, and offer biblical solutions that have helped many find greater freedom.

As we pray into our own lives or the lives of others, it is always wise to have a good understanding of our own history with Jesus and the history of those we are praying for. If our relationship with Jesus is based on a traditional or cultural understanding of who he is, then we may not have a relationship with him as Lord and Savior. When our relationship with Jesus is a "church thing," then it may not be an intimate or even a personal relationship on our part.

Belonging to a church is no surety of a relationship with the Lord of "the church," no matter how long we attended or how often we go to the services. With Jesus Christ, we need to be in a relationship that is personal, responsible, and responsive. Our relationships are based on a choice that we have made, not a choice of our parents or culture. Nationality or birth family is not a choice, but Christianity is always a personal choice.

When and how the decision was made to follow Jesus as Lord and Savior is significant. This can be a one time event that impacts us in such a profound way that it is a landmark experience. It can also be a series of progressive dedications that confirm our commitment to Jesus as our Lord and Savior.

For those of us who minister to others, there is a need to listen and look for the voice and the move of Holy Spirit to give "revelation" that will help us in the ministry. We need to hear from God as we listen to the one we are ministering to, just as Jesus saw and heard "what the Father was doing." We must also be actively attentive to the voice of the Spirit.

It is so important that we be led by Holy Spirit, and the Word of God. *We need to know the Word of God, and the heart of God, walking in the certainty of the Father's love and compassion.* We need to become aware that the Father wants their healing more than we do.

Our weakness is not of concern to the Father as much as the condition of our heart towards the one we are praying for.

One of the things we can almost be sure of is that when we hear the presenting problem, we are seeing the fruit, the outworking of something much deeper. As we minister, we need to be aware that we must address the root without ignoring the presenting problem. We need to keep the person we are ministering to involved and taking ownership of the process.

Most of the time people are not aware of the source of their problem. They are often dealing with the presenting symptoms (the problem at hand) and not the cause. However, these symptoms often reveal where we have to look to find the root of the problem.

These roots are often deep and unnoticed; they are the way we live life and the expectations we have about how life will go for us. These expectations set the tracks for the choices we make. When the choices we make are ungodly, they keep us in the problem.

Our will, (the place of choosing) needs to be in agreement with God. God requires that my will (the choices I make) be in line with His will in order for His will to operate in my life. We can resist the will of God for our lives – to our own detriment.

> *Therefore I urge you, brethren, by the mercies of God, to present your bodies a living and holy sacrifice, acceptable to God, which is your spiritual service of worship. And do not be conformed to this world, but be transformed by the renewing of your mind, so that you may prove what the will of God is, that which is good and acceptable and perfect.*
> **Romans 12:1-2**

ONE

IMPEDIMENTS, HINDRANCES AND SNAGS TO HEALING

God's will for my life is that I walk in wholeness—spiritual, emotional, mental, volitional and physical.

When wholeness is not the case in my life, I must look for a cause that creates a block to the healing work of Jesus in my life. The causes may be varied and unique to each one of us, but some of the more familiar ones are presented in the pages that follow.

No Faith In Who Jesus Says He Is

> *"Who is the liar? It is the man who denies that Jesus is the Christ."* **1 John 2:22** *NIV*

Some people have heard of Jesus and know about Him, but refuse to believe in who he says he is. Therefore they cannot or will not receive Him as Lord and Savior and Healer. Refusal to believe in the healer is very often the major hurdle that will block healing.

> *"To the Jews who had believed him, Jesus said, 'If you hold to my teaching, you are really my disciples. Then you will know the truth, and the truth will set you free.'"* **John 8:31-32** *NIV*

"I am the way and the truth and the life. No one comes to the Father except through me." **John 14:6** NIV

PRAYER

LORD JESUS, I CHOOSE to acknowledge you as the only begotten son of God. I choose to believe that you are who you say you are: the Son of God and that you are the only way to the Father. By an act of my will, I now declare that you are Lord of my life and my Savior.

I DO SO, BECAUSE I confess that on my own I can do nothing that has any lasting value.

I CONFESS THAT I have tried to create a life outside of you and I have failed. I confess that my independence from you is a sin and I ask for your forgiveness for all the ways in which I have gone my own way apart from you and Father God.

I THANK YOU FOR your grace and the price you paid on the cross so that I may have eternal life. I declare your Lordship into every part of my being:

I ASK YOU TO BE LORD OF MY SPIRIT,
LORD OF MY MIND,
LORD OF MY WILL,
LORD OF MY EMOTIONS,
LORD OF MY BODY,
LORD OF MY BEHAVIOR,

LORD OF MY RELATIONSHIPS,
LORD OF MY FUTURE
LORD OF MY PAST and my present.
I DECLARE THIS INTO my spirit and into
the heavenlies.

No Faith In God, Unbelief

Some people have no faith in God. They may believe in God, but they do not believe God. Believing in God requires that we also believe what He says in his Word. When we live with skepticism about God's commitment to those whom He created, we are facing another major hurdle to fullness of life. Such an active lack of faith at the core of a person's being can be a learned unbelief through teaching, experience or logic. They create strongholds that block the healing we so desire and that God wants to release into our lives.

Healing requires faith, as the following scriptures clearly show:

Centurion
So Jesus went with them. He was not far from the house when the centurion sent friends to say to him: "Lord, don't trouble yourself, for I do not deserve to have you come under my roof. That is why I did not even consider myself worthy to come to you. But say the word, and my servant will be healed... When Jesus heard this, he was amazed at him, and turning to the crowd following him,

he said, "I tell you, I have not found such great faith even in Israel." Then the men who had been sent returned to the house and found the servant well. **Luke 7:6-10** NIV

Syrophoenician woman

... She begged Jesus to drive the demon out of her daughter. ...Then he told her, "For such a reply, you may go; the demon has left your daughter." She went home and found her child lying on the bed, and the demon gone. **Mark 7:26-30** NIV

Woman with Issue of Blood

Just then a woman who had been subject to bleeding for twelve years came up behind him and touched the edge of his cloak. She said to herself, "If I only touch his cloak, I will be healed." Jesus turned and saw her. "Take heart, daughter," he said, "your faith has healed you." And the woman was healed from that moment. **Matthew 9:20-22** NIV

Demonized boy

A man in the crowd answered, "Teacher, I brought you my son, who is possessed by a spirit that has robbed him of speech. ...
Bring the boy to me."So they brought him. When the spirit saw Jesus, it immediately threw the boy into a convulsion. He fell to the ground and rolled around, foaming at the mouth. Jesus asked the boy's father, "How long has he been like this?" "From childhood," he answered...
But if you can do anything, take pity on us and help us." "'If you can'?" said Jesus. "Everything is possible for him who believes. Immediately the boy's father exclaimed, "I do believe; help me overcome my unbelief!" When Jesus saw that a crowd was running

to the scene, he rebuked the evil spirit. "You deaf and mute spirit," he said, "I command you, come out of him and never enter him again."
The spirit shrieked, convulsed him violently and came out." **Mark 9:17-26** *NIV*

Unbelief Blocks Healing

And He could do no work of power there, except that He laid His hands on a few sick ones, He healed them. And He marveled because of their unbelief. **Mark 6:4-6** *MKJV*

> **We all have faith in something. It is in what or whom we base our faith that is the important thing.**

Bargaining with God

Most of our faith says, "God may do something for me if I do something for Him…"

If we believe that we must earn God's favor, we may soon find out that we never quite measure up. Or we believe that through our own efforts we have earned a right to demand something from God. Both attitudes reveal a lack of understanding or even a lack of experience of the Father's heart towards us. When we fail to understand that His plans are never to harm, but to prosper, we will operate in striving, doubt and even fear of God.

Then the belief becomes that, "I must appease God" to get him to grant me the favor I seek.

We all have faith in something. It is what or whom we base our faith in that is the important thing. Some people place more faith in medicine or doctors for healing than God. We need to find out in what or in whom their faith rests.

> *And without faith it is impossible to please Him, for he who comes to God must believe that He is and that He is a rewarder of those who seek Him.* **Hebrews 11:6**

PRAYER

LORD GOD, I CONFESS that I have failed to believe your word. I have believed a lie that, although you are real, you don't really care about me.

I BELIEVED THAT THE promises of scripture are only for those few who have done all that is required for your blessings to flow to them.

I CONFESS AND REPENT for not believing that you truly love me. I confess and repent for believing that you will not help me unless I do those things that will cause you to love and care for me.

I CONFESS AND REPENT for living in the belief that your love has to be earned and that your love is conditional.

I CONFESS AND REPENT for believing that it was hopeless to try to please you and that you could never be pleased with me.

I NOW CHOOSE TO start trusting in your desire to bless me and love me unconditionally.

No Saving Knowledge Of Jesus

Some people may not know or want to know Jesus as Lord and Savior. They may want God to deal with the symptom, but not have any desire for a relationship with God.

God may heal the unbeliever to confirm who he says he is. This is a sign of His goodness and His presence so that the person may come to repentance and salvation.

Some have knowledge of Jesus, but have no faith that he will heal them. Others will say, "Yes, God heals," but (then) do not believe He will heal *them*. They somehow feel that for whatever reason they do not qualify for God's healing or grace. They never have experienced the love of the one who created them and died for them.

These are those who feel that they are not good enough to deserve God's mercy. By their belief they declare that they are disqualified from God's grace.

Unaware or unwilling to accept that God has always known of their state, they believe that they are not lovable, that they are outcasts, thereby labeling themselves as unclean and untouchable even by God.

But God demonstrates His own love toward us, in that while we were yet sinners, Christ died for us. **Romans 5:8**

When the belief that we must be good enough for God is rooted in us, we are disqualified by default. The first healing that may need to happen is in the area of our self–imposed disqualification.

There needs to be a revelation at the core of our being that we belong and are accepted by the Father through our Lord Jesus Christ.

Believing that we are genuine heirs of the Kingdom is often harder to believe than anything else.

Without a deep sense of belonging and knowing that we are acceptable through Christ Jesus, there will be a great struggle to believe that God (or for that matter anyone else) would care, or do anything for us just because of who we are.

The Spirit Himself testifies with our spirit that we are children of God, and if children, heirs also, heirs of God and fellow heirs with Christ... **Romans 8:16-17**

We are acceptable and we belong to the household of God; we are co-heirs with Christ Jesus for all eternity.

Believing that we are genuine heirs of the Kingdom is often harder to believe than anything else. As heirs, we have some prerogatives. One of them is being able to approach the throne of grace with boldness. Boldness comes from knowing the source of that prerogative, and His affection for us. However, boldness can easily turn to arrogance when we believe that we have a right to demand or expect that which is an act of love and unmerited grace.

Every time we demand something from God we do so in a spirit of confrontation and it puts enmity between God and us. It will block the blessings and keep them from flowing into our lives.

Therefore let us draw near with confidence to the throne of grace, so that we may receive mercy and find grace to help in time of need. **Hebrews 4:16**

27

PRAYER

LORD, I CONFESS AND repent for my unbelief in your goodness towards me.

I NOW CHOOSE TO receive you into my life as my Savior and My Lord. I choose to receive you as my redeemer who shed his blood for me, who died for me and who opened the way to the Father for me.

I REPENT FOR BELIEVING that I do not belong to you or that you don't really care for me.

I REPENT FOR BELIEVING that I would never be good enough for you.

I REPENT FOR BELIEVING that you love others more than me.

I REPENT FOR COMING to the conclusion that I am disqualified from your love, and therefore from your healing.

I REPENT FOR BELIEVING that because I am not good enough, have not done enough, nor prayed enough, I don't qualify as being acceptable in your sight.

I CONFESS, LORD JESUS, that I have no idea of who you are or how much you love me. Instead, I decided how lovable and how worthwhile I am rather than allowing you to tell me.

I CHOOSE TO RECEIVE your truth about me into my spirit, soul and body.

AND I THANK YOU for loving me into life.

No Belief That Jesus Heals

"And they took offense at him. But Jesus said to them, 'Only in his hometown and in his own house is a prophet without honor.' And he did not do many miracles there because of their lack of faith." **Matthew 13:57-58** NIV

Jesus was blocked by their lack of faith, and *our* lack of faith blocks healing. Jesus wanted to heal, to do miracles, but the community's lack of faith stopped it.

Our familiarity with Jesus can create a track of unbelief in us that is hard to break. Familiarity can create unbelief, not unlike the people in his own community. They saw him as they saw themselves and thought they knew all about him. Our culture and our faith community have more often than not defined Jesus for us as the God of yesterday and tomorrow, but who is not available to be with us in

29

> **We often have more faith in medicine than we have in God**

all his greatness today. When we believe that we understand who he is, what he can do, and can't or won't do, we are presuming and will miss the mark. Any understanding that is not based on the truth can block us in a number of ways, especially in the area of healing.

We often have more faith in medicine and what the world can do than we have in God. Medicine is a gift from God, but it does not replace him. It always seems easier to trust that which is at hand, placing our trust in the doctors rather than putting our faith in "The God who Heals you," Jehovah–Rapha. This does not mean that we reject the use of medicine and those who practice it, but that we do not make it our first choice.

Some people believe and teach that healing is not for today. They believe that healing and miracles only took place in the apostolic age of the church as a means to establish the church, declaring that God *did* heal in the past, but that He does not do so today. However, scripture is clear that He does not change.

> *Jesus Christ is the same yesterday and today and forever.* **Hebrews 13:8**

Our beliefs, when contrary to God, can effectively block God.

What we believe will affect our healing.

Some people may be in a church like the one described in Matthew.

> *And when He had come into His own country, He taught them in their synagogue, so much so that they were astonished and said, From where does this man have this wisdom and these mighty works?*
>
> *Is not this the carpenter's son? Is not his mother called Mary? And his brothers, James and Joses and Simon and Judas, and his sisters, are they not all with us? Then from where does this man have all these things? And they were offended in Him. But Jesus said to them, A prophet is not without honor, except in his own country and in his own house. And He did not do many mighty works there because of their unbelief.*
>
> **Matthew 13:54-58** MKJV

They may be so familiar with Jesus that they can't see Him for who he is. Their familiarity with the historical Jesus has become a channel for their lack of faith that can easily become a stronghold.

PRAYER

> *LORD JESUS, I COME to you to repent for believing that you no longer want to heal or minister into the life of your people.*

I CONFESS AND REPENT for that belief and choose to agree with your word. Your word states that you never change, that you are the same as you were in the beginning, you are the same today, and you will be the same tomorrow, next week, next month, next year and forever.

I CHOOSE TO BELIEVE in your constancy, in your unchanging nature. I choose to trust that truth and live in it from this day forward.

Two

Presumption In Prayer And Life

When we presume, we suppose that we know the truth of something without direct or positive proof; we are relying on what we assume is the truth. It can become a stubborn conviction where we declare that we know the heart and mind of God.

There is a tendency in the body of Christ to presume certain things about the character or nature of God. Our beliefs about Him, which may be and often are faulty, result in our thinking we can believe and do whatever we would like. We believe that God will understand and overlook our tendency to mold him into our image or shape him to fit our needs.

Presuming On God's Goodness

> *"Shall we sin because we are not under law but under grace? By NO MEANS!"* **Romans 6:15** NIV

> *"He who has been stealing must steal no longer, but must work."* **Ephesians 4:28** NIV

There may be a presuming upon God's grace, as Paul mentions in above passage in Romans, believing that, "God will overlook my behavior." Or even that, "God is love and therefore would never let anyone go to hell." Or still "God understands my need and therefore will overlook my offense."

This attitude, which seems more prevalent than not, results in a lifestyle that is out of balance and out of the will of God, presuming upon His grace all the while neglecting His holiness.

When we are out of balance with the ways of God, we are diseased. When we sin we bring trauma to our spirit, and affect our soul and body. Healing is needed to bring us into restoration.

> *Therefore confess your sins to each other and pray for each other so that you may be healed. The prayer of a righteous man is powerful and effective.* **James 5:16** NIV

Prayers of power require righteousness to release them. Without righteousness our lives quickly go out of balance. Our lives require Godly stability in all parts; any sinful activity brings an imbalance, which can and will harm us. We need to deal vigorously with any of our presumptions about God and his ways through repentance and forgiveness.

> *"Be very careful, how you live--not as unwise but as wise, making the most of every opportunity, because the days are evil. Therefore do not be foolish, but understand what the Lord's will is."* **Ephesians 5:15-17** NIV

PRAYER

LORD JESUS, I ASK you to forgive me for presuming upon your goodness, your mercy and your grace.

I HAVE PRESUMED THAT I have no responsibility for sin in my life. I believed that you would overlook my rebellion and allow me to walk in arrogance and presumption.

I CONFESS THAT THIS is sin and I repent for it.

I TRUST YOUR WORD that declares that if I repent and confess, you will forgive me and cleanse me from my sinfulness.

I THANK YOU, LORD, for your mercy towards me. I choose by an act of my will to walk in obedience and humility to your words.

I DECLARE THAT I have held you in contempt for not honoring you with my life and my behavior. I ask you for your forgiveness and cleansing.

THANK YOU LORD.

Praying For The Wrong Thing

This may be one of the most common reasons why people are not healed or set free.

When we are asked to pray for someone we need to ask the Lord what it is that he wants us to pray for in this situation. I have had occasions where someone has come asking for prayer into a specific issue when the Lord has not released me to do so. In this situation we can pray that the Lord bless them, but not pray for the presenting problem. This is not an easy thing to do, but if God does not release us we can't do it without moving in presumption.

Those who pray may even make statements on behalf of God presuming that it is God's will that they would be healed at that moment; this often comes from their soulish compassion on behalf of the one for whom they pray. There are times when God has not finished dealing with some issue in their lives and he is using the presenting problem as a way to draw them out of the place they are in to where he wants them to be.

When we do not seek God before we pray, our prayers can easily become presumptuous. Then our prayers are not out of the heart of God, but out of the heart of man, presuming we know God's will in a situation.

Frequently we are praying into the fruit not the root. Keep checking with God to learn if you are praying into the right thing.

PRAYER

LORD JESUS, I CONFESS that I have prayed with my mind and have not sought your wisdom and direction.

I CONFESS THAT I have prayed into what I thought was your heart and will. By doing this I have presumed to know the heart of God.

I ASK FOR YOUR forgiveness and release from any anger or resentment I have held towards you, my God, for not doing it my way.

I THANK YOU, LORD, for forgiving and cleansing me.

Three

A Bitter Heart: Moving From Sorrow To Healing

Bitterness is often the result of intense sorrow or painful affliction that can lead to extreme resentment, a grudge holding and hatred.

Once the resentment is established, it will lock our emotions in an entrenched position where bitterness begins to rule our lives. Therefore, the scripture admonishes us to deal with it so that we do not miss the grace and mercy of God.

> *Let no unwholesome word proceed from your mouth, but only such a word as is good for edification according to the need of the moment, so that it will give grace to those who hear. Do not grieve the Holy Spirit of God, by whom you were sealed for the day of redemption.* **Let all bitterness and wrath and anger and clamor and slander be put away from you, along with all malice.** *Be kind to one another, tenderhearted, forgiving each other, just as God in Christ also has forgiven you.* **Ephesians 4:29-32**

See to it that no one comes short of the grace of God; that no root of bitterness springing up causes trouble, and by it many be defiled; that there be no immoral or godless person like Esau, who sold his own birthright for a single meal. **Hebrews 12:15-16**

A root of bitterness is a dangerous condition of the spirit that will not only lead to the defilement of others, but also to error, or even breaks in relationships. It will even cause a person to withdraw from or even abandon commitments or previously acknowledged truth.

Unforgiveness

This is one of the most powerful areas of blockage.

"And when you stand praying, if you hold anything against anyone, forgive him so that your Father in heaven may forgive you of your sins." **Mark 11:25**

Forgiveness affects our healing. It is our choice to release, and not hold on to the hurts we experienced. It does not mean we forget, but it means that we refuse to bring it up, or to hold it against another or self. Without forgiveness we are still tied to the person and the event that wounded us.

The one who carries the hurt is bound to the past; the one who carries the hurt is tormented.

Unforgiveness is not changed by time; it binds us to the past.

Unforgiveness blocks healing; it gives the enemy a place to operate in our lives.

> *"In your anger do not sin: Do not let the sun go down while you are still angry, and do not give the devil a foothold."* **Ephesians 4:26**

When we don't forgive others or ourselves, we are in effect disobeying God and giving the enemy a right to harass and invade our lives. When we don't forgive ourselves, we may think that we are being holy, but by saying, *"God, I need to be punished more"* we are essentially declaring that the Cross is not enough for our sin.

When we minister we need to check and see if the forgiveness is real. Sometimes people will say they have forgiven, but in reality have chosen not to think about the offense or the pain anymore. However, every time the memory surfaces all the pain and anger are still present. When we have forgiven, it does not mean that there will not be some residual pain or fear as the healing is taking hold, but the pain cannot be as strong now as it was at the time of the event.

How a person sees themselves or the one who sinned against them is significant in determining the depth of the healing. Can they revisit the event without the bitterness or the pain that was there at the start? When healed, the person should be able to do this.

Look also for self-deception, particularly in the area of self-forgiveness. We may have forgiven everyone else, but may not have forgiven ourselves. This can easily create blockages in our life. The unforgiveness of self not only blocks healing, but it separates us from the love of the Father and those around us.

Our sin is not as offensive as our unwillingness to receive his mercy and grace. God is well aware of our weakness, but our inability to forgive ourselves is rooted in pride, and God opposes the proud.

Specific events and memories must be dealt with for fullness of healing to take place. Never allow someone to minimize an event in their life when Holy Spirit points it out as an issue that is holding them back. When we minimize or trivialize an event in our lives, we may be trying to avoid looking at something that carries with it pain and unresolved grief.

As we work through the forgiveness of others for specific events in our lives, it is very important we also ask the Lord to forgive us for our ungodly responses to the events. As this takes place, the witness to the confession declares that forgiveness has been accomplished, by stating to the person that they are forgiven: **1 John 1:9.**

> **Our inability to forgive ourselves is rooted in pride, and God opposes the proud.**

Declaring forgiveness into the person is very important. When the accuser comes to question their forgiveness or repentance, the person can declare that there is a witness to the event and therefore the matter is dealt with and established.

"But if he does not listen to you, take one or two more with you, so that BY THE MOUTH OF TWO OR THREE WITNESSES EVERY FACT MAY BE CONFIRMED. **Matthew 18:16**

Forgiveness does not deal with the emotions, but it gives the emotions an opportunity to be healed. The buried emotions attached to the event may surface, revealing the depth of the memory and the pain. But that does not mean that the forgiveness or repentance was not real. It only means that the emotions are coming to the surface and can now be dealt with in a proper manner.

"Therefore confess your sins to each other and pray for each other so that you may be healed. The prayer of a righteous man is powerful and effective." **James 5:16** *NIV*

Look for levels of forgiveness. Unforgiveness blocks God's healing in our lives; it says that, "I want justice and I will get it."

By holding on to the offense, we are in effect denying God's access to the situation. This can keep Him from bringing His justice into the event.

Peter came to Jesus and asked, "Lord, how many times shall I forgive my brother or sister who sins against me? Up to seven times?"

Jesus answered, "I tell you, not seven times, but seventy-seven times. **Matthew 18:21-22** NIV

Unforgiveness is defiling and carries consequences. We are forgiven much and if we don't act in a similar manner, we are open to the consequences of our lack of mercy. Like the servant in the parable.

> *Then the master called the servant in. 'You wicked servant,' he said, 'I canceled all that debt of yours because you begged me to. Shouldn't you have had mercy on your fellow servant just as I had on you?' In anger his master turned him over to the jailers to be tortured, until he should pay back all he owed. This is how my heavenly Father will treat each of you unless you forgive your brother from your heart."* **Matthew 18:32-35** NIV

Check for any roots of bitterness: those memories that keep us holding on to the offenses we experienced in relationships and events of life. They will defile us and defile others and keep us from fullness of life.

Ultimately, bitterness and unforgiveness go hand in hand; where there is no bitterness, forgiveness has been accomplished. Where there is unforgiveness we will find a root that goes deep and draws its life from a well of bitterness entrenched in our soul.

44

"Do not be deceived, God is not mocked; for whatever a man sows, this he will also reap."
Galatians 6:7

Bitterness is a deep-rooted, often hidden well of poison; it releases rebellion against the Word of God and hostility towards others. It controls us, holding us in bondage to our emotions and the one who harmed us.

One way to test for a spirit of bitterness is to think about the event or the one who hurt us. If we can keep a pure heart in the process, then we are well on our way to being healed in this specific area. If, however, we find that anger and resentment are still present, we may have to extend more forgiveness to the one who hurt us.

We can also ask Holy Spirit to bring to remembrance any event that still carries hidden bitterness in the heart. Forgiveness may not be completely done at one time; the event may have layers of pain that sometimes need to be addressed one at a time. But once the process is underway, God will release the layers in ways that we can manage, as we work through into forgiveness and freedom.

PRAYER

LORD, I CONFESS THAT I have carried and continue to carry bitterness and unforgiveness in my heart.

I CONFESS THAT I have failed to trust you with the injustices that have come against me or those I love.

I CONFESS THAT I have dwelled on the feeling of revenge and taken delight in the suffering of those who have caused me or those I love to suffer.

I ASK YOU, LORD, to forgive me for not being obedient to your word, which commands me to forgive so that I may be forgiven.

I NOW CHOOSE TO forgive those who have wronged me or those I love and release them into your hands.

I ASK FOR YOUR forgiveness for the bitterness I have carried in my heart and the bitterness I have spoken into others.

I THANK YOU, LORD, that you are a forgiving God. I thank you that you do forgive me and that through your forgiveness I am free from the curse of bitterness and unforgiveness.

I ASK YOU NOW, Lord, to cleanse me from the consequences of the unforgiveness and bitterness in my life.

Murmuring, Grumbling And Complaining

This often seems to be one of our favorite pastimes. We find fault, criticize, malign and complain. It seems to be almost second nature to us; we are not even aware of the destruction we are releasing into our lives or the lives of others.

> *As for the men whom Moses sent to spy out the land and who returned and made all the congregation grumble against him by bringing out a bad report concerning the land, even those men who brought out the very bad report of the land died by a plague before the* LORD. **Numbers 14:36-37**

It is a dangerous thing to murmur and complain. This does not mean that we don't recognize and confront a sinful situation, but we do it in a way that brings life to that situation by resolving the problem, rather than bringing division and offense to God through our murmuring.

Our words are a source of life and death. We can easily obstruct the healing of God for our lives by the words we speak. If there is a critical attitude, it can bring on the opposite of what we are looking for from God. A critical tongue has the power of death on it. It releases death from the person and into the person.

*Death and life are in the power of the
tongue, And those who love it will eat its
fruit.* **Proverbs 18:21**

Complaining about how unfair life is, or how God
does not seem to care, will create division between
God and us. This passage in Numbers brings this
home in a powerful way.

*Miriam and Aaron began to talk against
Moses because of his Cushite wife, for he had
married a Cushite. "Has the Lord spoken
only through Moses?" they asked. "Hasn't he
also spoken through us?" And the Lord
heard this. At once the Lord said to Moses,
Aaron and Miriam, "Come out to the tent
of meeting, all three of you." So the three of
them went out. Then the Lord came down in
a pillar of cloud; he stood at the entrance to
the tent and summoned Aaron and Miriam.
When the two of them stepped forward, The
anger of the Lord burned against them, and
he left them. When the cloud lifted from
above the tent, Miriam's skin was leprous—
it became as white as snow. Aaron turned
toward her and saw that she had a defiling
skin disease, and he said to Moses, "Please,
my lord, I ask you not to hold against us the
sin we have so foolishly committed. Do not let
her be like a stillborn infant coming from its
mother's womb with its flesh half eaten
away."* **Numbers 12:1-2,4-5, 9-12** NIV

*Do all things without murmurings and
disputings, so that you may be blameless and
harmless, the sons of God, without rebuke,*

48

in the midst of a crooked and perverse nation. Among these you shine as lights in the world, **Philippians 2:14-15** MKJV

We are encouraged by the word of God to take control over our words and thoughts so that things may go well for us.

> *For, "the one who desires life, to love and see good days, must keep his tongue from evil and his lips from speaking deceit. He must turn away from evil and do good; he must seek peace and pursue it. For the eyes of the Lord are toward the righteous, and his ears attend to their prayer, but the face of the lord is against those who do evil."* **1Peter 3:10-12**

PRAYER

LORD, I CONFESS TO murmuring and complaining. This seems to be a part of me that I make central in my life.

I AGREE WITH YOU that it is sin. I repent for participating in it and for initiating it.

I REPENT FOR THE words I have spoken in my murmuring and complaining.

I RECOGNIZE THAT THIS has defiled others and opened me up to the enemy.

I REPENT FOR BRINGING division into my relationship with others in the body of Christ and the community at large.

I ASK YOU, LORD, to release me from the consequences of my words and the ungodly agreements I entered into through these actions.

I ALSO CHOOSE TO forgive those who participated with me in these activities.

THANK YOU, LORD, THAT you cleanse me from my sin through your shed blood and death on the cross.

Four

Ungodly Attachments

We live in a world where the attachments we develop for people or things can and often do displace God in our lives.

These attachments are the people or the objects we can't seem to live without; they are our first love, those things for which we sacrifice family, friends, time, energy and money. They are the idols that rob us of the relationships and things that have eternal value.

When we value anything above God or Godly relationships, we are moving into ungodly attachments, and these attachments give the enemy a foothold in our lives.

We heard of a situation where a child damaged a parent's new car and the parent's first concern was for the condition of the car rather than the child's condition. This is an ungodly attachment.

We can have the same ungodly attachments to people whom we bring into our lives for our personal gratification or need to belong. When this happens we open the door for major demonic influences in our lives.

Ungodly Soul-Ties

Ungodly soul ties are formed through many types of sinful relationships. However, the most damaging are ones formed through ungodly sexual ties. These ties are created through any form of sexual activity that is outside marriage or any defiling sexual activity within marriage. Even though these are the most powerful of ties, they are not the only ways that damaging ties can be formed.

Ungodly ties can exist in a family, in the work place or in a social setting. Whenever we are in a relationship, long term or short term, there is always an occasion for a soul tie. These ties may not be harmful in any way, but the potential for a sinful bond to develop is always present.

However, there are many relationships that function mostly from a sinful attitude where all talk and activity is defiling and ungodly. They can happen when we join any group or organization that has an ungodly view or asks its members to take vows that are ungodly.

Even the places where we go for entertainment and the people we associate with in that place can be the source of ungodly ties.

Soul ties by their very nature were meant to be life giving. Finding a place in the life and heart of another can be nurturing, healing and freeing. They are meant to move us into fullness of life.

Ungodly ties are, by their very nature, life taking and are therefore damaging to relationships and the people in them. The harm caused by these relationships can have a life long effect that has to be healed. Any soul tie that has negatively impacted our lives needs to be dealt with through repentance, forgiveness and prayers to break them.

Ties That Bind

Soul ties always exist between sexual partners. A husband and wife relationship which is blessed by God forms an incredible life giving tie.

> *"For this reason a man will leave his father and mother and be united to his wife, and they will become one flesh.* **Genesis 2:24** NIV

However, even in a relationship that is blessed by God there is a potential for the formation of ungodly ties. These can easily be formed when the use of the sexual relationship becomes a means of control by either partner through defilement, manipulation, intimidation or domination in the relationship.

They can become ungodly and defiling when sinful means are used to stimulate one or both of the partners through the use of literature or audio/visual material.

Any sexual relation outside of marriage, no matter what the circumstances, creates an ungodly bond, or soul tie.

> *Do you not know that your bodies are members of Christ himself? Shall I then take the members of Christ and unite them with a prostitute? Never! Do you not know that he who unites himself with a prostitute is one with her in body? For it is said, "The two will become one flesh."* **1 Corinthians 6:15-16** NIV

We can have Godly soul ties with friends.

> *After David had finished speaking with Saul, Jonathan became one in spirit with David, and he loved him as himself.*
> **1 Samuel 18:1** NIV

> **"***...that their (believers) hearts may be encouraged, having been knit together in love...* **" Colossians 2:2**

We need to be ever mindful that all relationships have the potential to become ungodly. When friendship becomes controlling, the relationship tie has become ungodly.

There are soul ties between parents and children.

> *"So now, if the boy is not with us when I go back to your servant my father, and if my father whose life is closely bound up with the boy's life, sees that the boy isn't there, he will die."* **Genesis 44:30-31**

Soul ties can exist between people and their leaders.

> *So all the men of Israel withdrew from*
> *following David, and followed Sheba the son*
> *of Bichri; but the men of Judah remained*
> *steadfast to their king, from the Jordan even*
> *to Jerusalem.* **2 Samuel 20:2**

Soul ties can be formed with institutions, by entering into covenant relationships:

> *"Watch yourself that you make no covenant*
> *with the inhabitants of the land into which*
> *you are going, lest it become a snare in your*
> *midst. . . and you take some of his daughters*
> *for your sons, and his daughters play the*
> *harlot with their gods, and cause your sons*
> *also to play the harlot with their gods."*
> **Exodus 34:12-16**

Ungodly soul ties need to be dealt with through confession, repentance and renunciation, and then broken.

Ungodly ties, particularly sexual ties, can carry with them guilt, shame and self-condemnation. As prayer ministers, we need to be very conscious and sensitive of other people's need for privacy and safety.

This is particularly true of those who have been victimized through any form of sexual abuse. Sexual abuse can occur through a word or a look; any time a person feels sexually defiled it is a form of abuse.

When we minister to others, we need to deal with sexual sin and the soul ties formed as a result of these ungodly relationships. We also need to deal with the guilt, shame, fear, or powerlessness often associated with it that may result in low self-esteem, anger at self and one's sexual partner.

We also need to have the person renounce the pleasure that drew them into the sin. If sin had no gratification, or the prospect of gratification, we would not be easily tempted. However, where the person was violated particularly through rape (in or outside of marriage) the anger and the hatred need to be renounced.

PRAYER

LORD JESUS, I CONFESS and repent for any ungodly relationship in which I have been involved.

I CHOOSE TO FORGIVE those who have used me and abused me.

I REPENT FOR THE times used or abused people.

I REPENT FOR ALLOWING others to control me through fear or manipulation. I choose to forgive those who have done this to me.

I REPENT FOR COMING into agreement with those who were acting sinfully because I wanted to belong or profit from their associations.

I REPENT FOR THE relationships that were based on sexual pleasure outside of your covenant. I forgive those who participated in them with me.

LORD, I NOW ASK you to cut all the ungodly linkages between me and these people. I pray that there is no longer a hold of any kind in my life to those ungodly connections.

I RELEASE EACH AND every person who has violated my Godly integrity.

I ASK YOU TO forgive me and release me from each and every person whose integrity and dignity I have violated. I ask you to bless them and heal them through the power of your Name.

Five

Trauma And Fear

Trauma comes from the Greek word for "wound;" when we are traumatized we are wounded, whether it is in the spirit, soul or body. The wounding that takes place in those areas causes distress to enter our lives.

Where there is wounding there is a need for healing and sanctification.

> *Now may the God of peace Himself sanctify you entirely; and may your spirit and soul and body be preserved complete, without blame at the coming of our Lord Jesus Christ.* **1 Thessalonians 5:23**

We must not forget that any form of trauma can be considered a wound, whether to our spirit, to our soul (mind, will or emotions) or to our body. The most recognizable form of trauma is that which happens to the body through injury or violence. This includes surgery (controlled trauma), no matter how minor.

What is often unrecognized is that any impact or invasion of the body brings trauma to the spirit and soul. Our soul can be just as traumatized through violation to our emotions, our will and our mind. However, this form of trauma is often ignored.

There is another form of trauma which happens to our spirits that is even more impacting. Often it is given very little attention in the process of healing.

The spirit is traumatized by sin: the sin we commit, the sin that is committed against us, or the sin we witness through others.

One thing is certain: trauma is a major demonic access point.

Since we are triune beings (spirit, soul and body), when one part of us is traumatized the other parts are also impacted. We must minister into all three parts, focusing on the primary source of the trauma, and from there to the other two parts. Therefore, if a person has been physically violated, we not only minister to the body, but also to the spirit and the soul.

Dissociation is a very specialized area of ministry. It should only be done by those who are called by God and have received training in this area.

One of the results of major trauma, whether accidental or intentional, can be dissociation where a person buries the memory of the trauma in their subconscious. They go on with life often not remembering the trauma of the event.

Note: This is a very poor explanation, but this book is not meant to   address this issue. There is some excellent material available today   that deals in great depth on this subject.

PRAYER

LORD JESUS, YOU KNOW all that has taken place at every moment in my life.

I THANK YOU THAT through your grace and mercy you have kept the enemy from totally destroying me.

I DID NOT UNDERSTAND why certain things were happening to me. In the process, I judged and accused you of not caring.

LORD, I ASK YOU to forgive me for blaming you for all that went wrong in those times of trauma in my life.

I BREAK THE POWER of the accuser who keeps telling me that you, Lord, do not care.

I ASK YOU TO forgive me for believing his lie. Lord, I choose to look at the cross on which you died for me, so that I may have eternal life.

I NOW CHOOSE TO forgive those who through their actions, or failure to act, brought trauma into my life.

I FORGIVE THOSE WHO for their pleasure or lack of caring caused me great pain.

I THANK YOU THAT I do not remember all that has taken place, but you, Lord, do remember.

AS I FORGIVE THOSE who hurt me--either through intent or through ignorance--I ask you, Lord, to forgive me for my judgments and curses.

I THANK YOU, LORD, that you are at work in me at this very moment to bring healing and life where destruction had been the enemy's goal.

I THANK YOU THAT you will never leave me or forsake me.

LORD, I NOW ASK you to bring into my life those who will help me walk through the pain and the trauma. Teach me to open my heart to trust you and people again.

I THANK YOU FOR your life and the grace you continue to extend to me in my journey to wholeness.

Fear

Fear is an emotion, often birthed through trauma, that brings a painful apprehension of some impending pain or evil which causes us to look for escape or security.

The way to break the power of the trauma and the subsequent fear is through love: the love of God and the love of others.

> *There is no fear in love; but perfect love casts out fear, because fear involves punishment, and the one who fears is not perfected in love.*
> *We love, because He first loved us...* **1 John 4:18-19**

> *"A new commandment I give to you, that you love one another, even as I have loved you, that you also love one another.*
> *"By this all men will know that you are My disciples, if you have love for one another."*
> **John 13:34-35**

However, we are not always operating in the place of love, or even living in the love of God and therefore we are often controlled by all kinds of fears and anxieties.

Being Controlled By Fear

Fear is one of the major tools the enemy uses to keep us in bondage. He uses whatever means he can to instill fear in us; once he accomplishes this, the fear becomes an access point for him to attack and control us.

The enemy uses fear to separate us from God. His goal is to block us from the freedom and healing Jesus died to give us. If he can convince us that God is angry with us, or that we have to earn God's favor, we give him the right to fill us wth the very thing we fear.

When Adam and Eve ate from the tree of the knowledge of good and evil, they saw a reality that they had been protected from when they stayed in the will of God.

> "... I heard Your voice in the garden, and I was afraid because I was naked, so I hid."
> **Genesis 3:10-11** NIV

Whenever we feel exposed and vulnerable we can easily surrender to fear and move into a self-protective mode. When we begin to doubt our source of life, nothing feels safe and we will try to hide or run away. When fear enters our life the enemy has gained a major foothold.

> What the wicked fears shall come upon him; but the desire of the righteous shall be granted. **Proverbs 10:24**

> Peace I leave with you; my peace I give to you. I do not give to you as the world gives. Do not let your hearts be troubled and do not be afraid. **John 14:27** NIV

PRAYER

LORD JESUS, I CONFESS *that I have allowed fear to rule in my life.*

I HAVE ALLOWED FEAR *of others, fear of the future, and fear of looking foolish to stop me from doing what is right and proper.*

I DECLARE THAT I *have even shaped my life to avoid the fear and therefore have given fear precedence in my life even over you.*

I CHOOSE TO AGREE *with you that this spirit of fear is not from you, but from the enemy.*

YOU HAVE NOT GIVEN *me "a spirit of timidity, but of power and love and discipline."*

THEREFORE I NOW REPENT *for having more faith in my fear than in your love and ability to sustain me through all trials and tribulations.*

I CHOOSE TO FORGIVE *those who were instruments of fear in my life, and I repent for submitting to that fear.*

THANK YOU, LORD JESUS *that there is no fear in you.*

THANK YOU FOR SETTING *me free from all the fear that has controlled my life.*

Unrecognized Abuse And Other Damage

Physical, sexual, verbal, emotional, and spiritual abuse can cause much damage. It is often not recognized as abuse by the person who is victimized.

This is particularly true where the abuse was part of a life style, where the ungodly behavior was considered "normal." In such situations the actions seemed to be a normal part of life. Some investigating by the prayer minister will soon reveal what the home life was like during the growing years.

"What was father like?"

"What was mother like?"

"How did the family, father and mother, spend time together?"

"How was discipline enforced?

"How was comfort given? Etc.

When correction or discipline offers little or no hope and assurance of a better future, it can and will cause damage to our personhood. Discipline must always be applied with a future good in mind. The person being disciplined must be made aware that this is ultimately for their own good and protection. Discipline should always be seen as a "surgical procedure" rather than a "wounding action."

PRAYER

LORD JESUS, THERE IS so much that has taken place in my life that I do not remember.

I ASK YOU NOW to bring to mind those things that still hold me in bondage. I ask you to break these bondages and heal the wounds caused by them.

I ALSO ASK YOU to heal those things that are harmful, and those which I do not need to remember to be healed.

LORD, YOU KNOW ALL that gives life. You died that I may be free from the things that do not bring life.

I AGREE WE DO not even realize that those things we do as a matter of course may be robbing us of the fullness of life that you came to give us through your death on the cross.

LORD, AS YOU MINISTER into those places in my life where I am even now unaware of being damaged, I choose to forgive those who were instrumental in causing that damage either through neglect or intentionally.

LORD, I ASK YOU to forgive me for the ways that I have through neglect or carelessness brought damage to my own life or the life of others.

Six

Rebellion and Defying God

Disobedience is open defiance against the will of God; it is an act of rebellion.

When we blatantly oppose the will of God, we disobey; we are in rebellion and God does not tolerate opposition to the very thing that will give us life: His word.

We see this in Saul's defiance of God's command.

> But Samuel replied: "For rebellion is like the sin of divination, and arrogance like the evil of idolatry. Because you have rejected the word of the Lord, he has rejected you as king." **1 Samuel 15:22,23**

Rebellion is in essence a declaration of war.

When we rebel against God we resist his lawful authority and disobey his commands. We are openly declaring that we renounce His authority and withdraw our loyalty to him.

Disobedience

Sin, known or unknown, is always defiance to his laws. Obedience to the laws of God keeps us safe and healthy. His laws are not only spiritual, but also moral and physical; they encompass every part of our lives. Ignorance of the law does not negate the law in any way and it is never an excuse for disobedience;

Indeed, when Gentiles, who do not have the law, do by nature things required by the law, they are a law for themselves, even though they do not have the law. They show that the requirements of the law are written on their hearts, their consciences also bearing witness, and their thoughts sometimes accusing them and at other times even defending them. **Romans 2:14-15**

"This is the covenant I will make with them thereafter that time says the Lord. I will put my laws in their hearts and will write them on their minds. **Hebrews 10:16**

Our ignorance does not protect us from the operation of that law. The laws <u>will work</u> whether we break them willingly or in ignorance. Breaking the law will always have consequences.

We are called to be obedient servants of the Lord. We find, however, that we often choose what we will and will not do, thereby moving into disobedience which is rebellion.

"Do not think that I came to abolish the Law of the Prophets; I did not come to abolish, but to fulfill them." **Matthew 5:17**
NIV

"Do not be deceived, God is not mocked; for whatever a man sows, this he will also reap."
Galatians 6:7

"...but each one is tempted when, by his own evil desire, he is dragged away and enticed. Then, after desire has conceived, it gives birth to sin; and sin, when it is full-grown, gives birth to death." **James 1:14-15** NIV

"Let no one deceive you with empty words, for because of such things God's wrath comes on those who are disobedient." **Ephesians 5:6** NIV

"See, I am setting before you today a blessing and a curse— the blessing if you obey the commands... the curse if you disobey the commands of the Lord your God" **Deuteronomy 11:26-27, 28** NIV

PRAYER

LORD, I CONFESS AND repent for my unwillingness to follow your commands in my life.

I CONFESS THAT I HAVE CHOSEN to be my own person apart from you and I have gone astray.

I ASK YOU TO forgive me for my stubbornness and rebellion. I ask you to forgive me for my pride and my independence.

I CONFESS THAT THROUGH my actions I have declared that I know better than you what I need and how to live my life.

I CONFESS THAT THROUGH these actions I have opened the door to the enemy and I have separated myself from your protection and guidance.

LORD, I REPENT AND ask for your grace to cleanse me from my sin.

TEACH ME, LORD, TO live according to your word.

TEACH ME, THAT I may live life as a true witness of your mercy and grace towards me.

Touching God's Anointed

We seem to live in a world that values independence more than commitment, a world that attaches more value to convenience than loyalty. We live in a society that delights in the critical tongue and suspects all who have been given authority over us.

There is a great tendency not only in the church, but also in the world to look for a way to find fault with our institutions and those who lead them. There is a certain delight in knowing and dwelling on the failures of those who are given or assigned to positions of authority. This is critically evident in the church where pastors and leaders are constantly judged and criticized for what they do or fail to do.

Yet, the word of the Lord is clear to us about the issue of the way we are to address and speak about those who have been given authority.

> *"...Do not touch my anointed ones; do my prophets no harm."* **Psalm 105:15** NIV

The story of David and Saul is a wonderful illustration of how to behave when we are being unjustly treated.

With David it was not just an issue of unfairness; it was a case of life and death.

He could have easily killed Saul and just as easily assumed the throne of Israel. However, David understood what so many fail to understand today, that God had anointed Saul and that no matter what God's promise to David was, David could not in any way force the outcome.

The relationship with Saul was fearful and painful, but David never ceased to honor and protect him. When Saul died, there was, as a result, no one who could claim that David had a part in it.

> *He said to his men, "The Lord forbid that I should do such a thing to my master, the Lord's anointed, or lay my hand on him; for*

he is anointed of the Lord." With these words David sharply rebuked his men and did not allow them to attack Saul. And Saul left the cave and went on his way. **1 Samuel 24:6-7;**
1 Samuel 26:9-10 NIV

And David said, Why were you not afraid to stretch forth your hand to destroy Jehovah's anointed? **2 Samuel 1:14** MKJV

Touching God's anointed carries a curse.

Touching can mean anything from a careless word to an overt plot to bring someone harm or to remove someone from a position of Godly authority.

Only God can deal with those in the place of authority.

Then Jesus spoke to the crowd and to His disciples, saying, The scribes and the Pharisees sit in Moses' seat. Therefore whatever they tell you to observe, observe and do. But do not do according to their works; for they say, and do not do.
For they bind heavy and hard-to-carry burdens and lay them on men's shoulders. But they will not move them with one of their fingers. **Matthew 23:1-4** MKJV

Let every soul be subject to the governing authorities, for there is no authority except that which God has established. Consequently, whoever rebels against the authority is rebelling against what God has

instituted. And those who do so will bring
judgment on themselves.
For rulers hold no terror for those who do
right, but for those who do wrong.
Let no debt remain outstanding, except for
the continuing debt of love for one another,
for whoever loves others has fulfilled the law.
Romans 13:1-3, 8 NIV

We are to pray for those who have authority over us, particularly when we are not in agreement with them. When we curse, we fail to honor those who are appointed over us. As a result of not honoring and protecting even through the words we speak, we can come under oppression and fail to discern the Lord in the person or the situation. This can create a major block to the move of God in our lives.

PRAYER

LORD JESUS, I CONFESS that I have
touched your anointed ones, whether they were
my parents, my teachers, my pastors, leaders in
the church and government. I have done so
through my words, my actions or inactions.

I HAVE DONE SO in my prayers and in the very
fellowship I attend, or attended in the past.

I FAILED TO HONOR them, and through that I failed to honor you, by not lifting them up in life-giving prayer.

I HAVE JUDGED, I have cursed. I have been self-righteous in my attitude towards those you put in authority.

I CONFESS THAT THROUGH my words and actions I have conspired and acted on my own sense of what is right and wrong. Those actions have brought a curse on my self and exposed those in leadership over me through my unrighteousness.

I ASK YOU, LORD, to forgive me and cleanse me and those I have maligned from the actions of my words and deeds.

I ASK YOU, LORD, to bless those I have cursed and bring life to those I proclaimed death to.

I THANK YOU, LORD, for your faithfulness and great mercy towards me.

Robbing God

When our children were growing up, they had no money to buy the things they wanted to give us for special occasions, so like good parents we provided the funds for them to buy us the gifts. We did not need the gifts, but it gave them a way to express their honor and love for us.

If we gave one of them $10.00 and they gave us a $1.00 gift it would cause us to wonder about their affection for us.

When God provides for us, He does not expect us to give it all back, but only that token which represents our honoring and affection for Him. However, when we fail to give back and keep from God all that is rightfully His, we declare that we do not trust Him and we move into rebellion.

> ## When we keep from God all that is rightfully His, we declare that we do not trust Him.

That which we keep from God begins to create a blockage for his move in our lives. When we give we open a door to a deeper and deeper relationship. The exchange of gifts has always meant to be a building block in relationships.

Giving has always been a part of God's plan for His people. We are not to hold on to the first fruits but dedicate them to the one who gave them to us.

> *Bring the whole tithe into the storehouse, that there may be food in my house. Test me in this, says the LORD Almighty, "and see if I will not throw open the floodgates of heaven and pour out so much blessing that there will not be room enough to store it. I will prevent pests from devouring your crops, and the vines in your fields will not drop their fruit before it is ripe," says the LORD Almighty. "Then*

all the nations will call you blessed, for yours will be a delightful land," says the LORD *almighty.* **Malachi 3:10-12** NIV

PRAYER

LORD, I CONFESS AND *repent for the ways in which I have failed to trust in your word and your provision.*

I CONFESS THAT I *have trusted in my finances more that in your ability to provide for all my needs.*

YOUR WORD DECLARES THAT *the whole world belongs to you and that all I have is from your hand.*

I NOW CHOOSE TO *trust you and not to rely upon my abilities to provide for myself.*

I THANK YOU THAT *you do provide a way for me to have an opportunity to give back to you through giving into the things of the kingdom.*

Seven

Blockages of Sin

"For the wages of sin is death, but the gift of God is eternal life in Christ Jesus our Lord." **Romans 6:23** NIV

"Therefore each of you must put off falsehood and speak truthfully to his neighbor, for we are all members of one body. 'In your anger do not sin': Do not let the sun go down while you are still angry, and do not give the devil a foothold." **Ephesians 4:25-27** NIV

Is any one of you sick? He should call the elders of the church to pray over him and anoint him with oil in the name of the Lord. And the prayer offered in faith will make the sick person well; the Lord will raise him up. If he has sinned, he will be forgiven. Therefore confess your sins to each other and pray for each other so that you may be healed. The prayer of a righteous man is powerful and effective. **James 5:14-16** NIV

Unconfessed sin is a major blockage to a Godly life and any kind of healing. It creates isolation from God in us and leaves us vulnerable to all kinds of deception; it also becomes a huge landing pad for the enemy.

Being our own judge of what is right and wrong is always dangerous. This is simply because we may not be able to see that our life style may be sinful.

Paul, a man of God, did not see anything sinful or unconfessed in himself, but still left the final decision up to God.

> Being our own judge of what is right and wrong is always dangerous.

> *For I am conscious of nothing against myself, yet I am not by this acquitted; but the one who examines me is the Lord. Therefore do not go on passing judgment before the time, but wait until the Lord comes who will both bring to light the things hidden in the darkness and disclose the motives of men's hearts; and then each man's praise will come to him from God.* **1 Corinthians 4:4-5**

So many people believe that their relationship with God is just fine, but they do not bother to check with Holy Spirit to learn if there are issues that are or will create problems in their lives.

David knew his heart and trusted God to reveal the things that lay buried deep inside him.

> *Search me, O God, and know my heart; Try me and know my anxious thoughts; And see if there be any hurtful way in me, And lead me in the everlasting way.* **Psalm 139:23-24**

There may be areas in our lives that have been buried since childhood. Those sinful things that we said and did in childhood, long forgotten by us and those around us, are not forgotten by God or by Satan.

Once we establish a pattern of behavior early on in life (and get away with it), it becomes a habit that we don't even realize is a sin. The Father, through Holy Spirit, brings us to an awareness of our sin, so that we can be set free.

Just as parents want their children to learn and take responsibility for their actions, our heavenly Father also wants us to acknowledge and learn from our sin.

Confession may feel like a humbling experience, but the power of it lies in the breaking and destroying the bridge that has allowed free access for the work of the enemy in our life.

Confession breaks the legal contract we have entered into with Satan. Confession releases us into God's forgiveness and frees us from condemnation.

PRAYER

LORD JESUS, I CONFESS that there are areas in my life where I have maintained an active resistance to your truth and your life.

I CONFESS THAT I have held on to besetting sin in my life. That I tried to explain it away, tried to justify it to myself and others, and even to you, Lord.

I NOW DECLARE THAT this sin robs me of life, dignity, integrity and your presence.

I PRAY THAT YOU forgive me and cleanse me of this sin, and choose to take responsibility for my actions.

NOW BY AN ACT of my will I choose to live a life that is worthy of your grace and mercy.

Flagrant Or Habitual Sin

When through corrupt habits developed early in life we learn to operate in a sinful manner, we may inadvertently open a door for the enemy to operate in our lives.

There are some sins that we commit on a regular basis feeling that we have immunity from the consequences, believing that somehow God will overlook this offense against him because he understands our needs.

> *Do not be deceived, God is not mocked; for whatever a man sows, this he will also reap. For the one who sows to his own flesh will from the flesh reap corruption, but the one who sows to the Spirit will from the Spirit reap eternal life. Let us not lose heart in doing good, for in due time we will reap if we do not grow weary.* **Galatians 6:7-9**

This is a momentous form of presumption that can and will create major blockages in our lives and even the lives of those we have responsibility for or authority over.

> *For the wages of sin is death, but the gift of God is eternal life through Jesus Christ our Lord.* **Romans 6:23** NIV

> *For the acts of the flesh are obvious: sexual immorality, impurity and debauchery, idolatry and witchcraft; hatred, discord, jealousy, fits of rage, selfish ambition, dissections, factions and envy; drunkenness, orgies and the like. I warn you, as I did before, that those who live like this will not inherit the kingdom of God.* **Galatians 5:19-21** NIV

In the preceding verses we can see Paul's solemn warning. As we explore each of the things he warns us about, we may find that some of them are a part of our lives in one form or another. When sin has it's veneer stripped away, it will be revealed to have its source in great darkness.

Flagrant or habitual sin can vary from sexual sin, gossip, criticism and lying, to stealing and a myriad of other activities or omissions that violate the nature of God.

One of the most flagrant and often overlooked sins is the sin of criticalness and gossip. If what we say or fail to say about someone causes others to see them in a negative light or to say things about them that are not life giving or honoring, then we have entered a dangerous area.

It seems that for the most part, the church and the Christian community at large have come to an acceptance of criticism and dishonoring of those in authority or those with whom we do not agree. The scripture is clear:

> *"The good man brings out of his good treasure what is good; and the evil man brings out of his evil treasure what is evil. But I tell you that every careless word that people speak, they shall give an accounting for it in the day of judgment. For by your words you will be justified, and by your words you will be condemned."* **Matthew 12:35**

Our words makes us susceptible to judgment. In addition, when we sin through our careless words, or critical thoughts, we may be creating stumbling blocks for the grace of God in our lives.

PRAYER

LORD JESUS, I CONFESS that there is a habitual way in me that is sinful; it is a flagrant disregard to your word and grace.

I CONFESS THAT I have not resisted to the place of dying to this sin in my life, and I confess its hold over me. I also declare that your word says that there is no sin that will tempt me for which you have not prepared a way to escape.

I DECLARE AND AGREE with your word that:

"NO TEST OR TEMPTATION that comes my way is beyond the course of what others have had to face. All I need to remember is that you, Lord God, will never let me down. You'll never let me be pushed beyond my limit. You'll always be there to help me come through it."

I THANK YOU, LORD, for your provision of escaping the sin that so besets me and damages my life.

I ASK FOR THE courage to face my sin and resist it as I submit to you.

THANK YOU FOR YOUR forgiveness and mercy to me.

Sins Of Ignorance

We have already addressed this at some length; however, we often still operate under the presumption that, "What I don't know can't hurt me." When our own hearts decide what is and what is not sinful we are walking a very dangerous path.

God has not left us in the dark or defenseless.

> *"But the Helper, the Holy Spirit, whom the Father will send in My name, He will teach you all things, and bring to your remembrance all that I said to you.* **John 14:26**

Ignorance of the law has never been an excuse for consequences to breaking the law. It may result in lenience, but is never an excuse. Whenever a law is broken there are consequences, either to us individually or to the community at large.

> *"The Lord said to Moses, 'Say to the Israelites: When anyone sins unintentionally and does what is forbidden in any of the Lord's commands... If the whole Israelite community sins unintentionally and does what is forbidden in any of the Lord's commands, even though the community is*

86

unaware of the matter, they are guilty."
Leviticus 4:2, 13 NIV

"If a person sins and does what if forbidden in any of the Lord's commands, even though he does not know it, he is guilty and will be held responsible." **Leviticus 5:17** NIV

"That servant who knows his master's will and does not get ready or does not do what his master wants will be beaten with many blows. But the one who does not know and does things deserving punishment will be beaten with few blows." **Luke 12:47-48** NIV

As the Lord reveals childhood sins, those sins need to be confessed. Our responses to events in our lives are either Godly or ungodly! We need constantly to remember that the Godly responses bring freedom, and the ungodly (sinful) responses will create bondage.

PRAYER

LORD JESUS, I CONFESS that there were times in my life when I acted in a way that was not wholesome. I confess that my behavior caused pain and distress to those around me.

I CONFESS THAT ON those occasions I acted in ways that were not pleasing to you or those around me. Even though I was not aware of it then, I now confess it as sin and ask you to forgive me for those things.

I ACKNOWLEDGE THAT THE enemy has used my ignorance to give him some inroads into my life.

I NOW ASK YOU to remove those rights through your shed blood on the cross.

I AGREE THAT IGNORANCE of the law is no excuse, so I agree with your law and confess and repent of my sins of ignorance.

LORD, YOU KNOW WHAT they are and so I ask for your forgiveness and I thank you for it.

AMEN.

Eight

Turning Away from God

Turning away from God seems to be something that is recurrent throughout all of scripture.

In scripture we also read of God's constant call to return and be safe. Every time we sin we turn away from God.

When we turn away we are saying that there is a better way or that we do not want to submit to His way. We want to do things which we believe are more advantageous to us. When we turn away from serving God we fail to realize that we are turning to serve another who only wants to "kill, rob and destroy."

Seek the LORD while He may be found; Call upon Him while He is near. Let the wicked forsake his way And the unrighteous man his thoughts; And let him return to the LORD, And He will have compassion on him, And to our God, For He will abundantly pardon. For My thoughts are not your thoughts, Nor are your ways My ways," declares the LORD. For as the heavens are higher than the earth, So are My ways higher than your ways And My thoughts than your thoughts. **Isaiah 55:6-7**

We turn away from God and begin seeking other forms of spiritual activities. One of the easiest one to fall into is the occult.

Occult Involvement

Any occult activity, even if entered into innocently, will create a spiritual blockage in our lives. When we willfully participate in occult activities, it forms a distorted perception of God in our lives. This will inevitably open us to aspects in the spiritual realm that will generate confusion and undermine our strength in Christ. As we minister we need to look where the confusion and weakness entered the person we are praying for, to help bring their life back into God's order.

While all rebellion is witchcraft, occult involvement is its most rebellious form.

Occult involvement is always a turning away from God; it is a declaration that we trust something else more than Him. While all rebellion is witchcraft, occult involvement is its most rebellious form. *It is a direct confrontation to the will of the Father, a purposeful alignment with the enemy.* This is a major blockage to Godly healing.

> *When you enter the land the Lord your God is giving you, do not learn to imitate the detestable ways of the nations there. Let no*

one be found among you who sacrifices their son or daughter in the fire, who practices divination or sorcery, interprets omens, engages in witchcraft, or casts spells, or who is a medium or spiritist or who consults the dead. Anyone who does these things is detestable to the Lord; because of these same detestable practices the Lord your God will drive out those nations before you. You must be blameless before the Lord your God.
The nations you will dispossess listen to those who practice sorcery or divination. But as for you, the Lord your God has not permitted you to do so. **Deuteronomy 18:9-14** NIV

PRAYER

LORD JESUS, I DECLARE that you and only you are the way to the Father.

I DECLARE THAT ALL other ways are traps and demonic deception.

I CONFESS AND REPENT for any and all ways in which I have been involved in the occult.

I AGAIN CONFESS MY unbelief in your word that warns me to stay away from such things.

LORD, WHERE I HAVE toyed with the occult, believing it was a harmless thing, I ask you to forgive me for ignoring your warning.

LORD, WHERE I HAVE used it to discern the future, believing that the enemy's methods were better, more accurate and more believable than your way, I repent.

LORD, I RENOUNCE MY trust in the ways of darkness. I choose to walk away from anything that does not come from you.

I THANK YOU, LORD, for your forgiveness and the cleansing that comes from the blood of Jesus.

Nine

Generational Influences

We tend to forget that the past has an effect on our lives today.

There is a saying that states, "Those who forget the past are condemned to relive it." There is truth in this. We are not to focus on the past, but if we do not deal with the legacy handed down to us from generations past, we will inevitably be caught up in the attitudes, beliefs and sins of those whose DNA we carry in our spirit, soul and body.

Generational Sin And / Or Demonization

We all have inherited the physical DNA from our parents that makes us who we are physically. We seldom, however, consider the possibility that we also have inherited the soul DNA (mind, will and emotions), and the spiritual DNA. We come into life with blessings and curses that we inherit from our ancestors.

Generational traits, character modeling, general attitudes and prejudices which are ungodly can be inherited from previous generations; curses and sinful patterns can be inherited as well. These can be a source of sin and a blockage to the blessings and healing that are rightfully ours in Christ Jesus.

> *"The Lord, the Lord, the compassionate and gracious God, slow to anger, abounding in love and faithfulness, maintaining love to thousands, and forgiving wickedness, rebellion and sin. Yet he does not leave the guilty unpunished; he punishes the children and their children for the sin of the fathers to the third and fourth generation."* **Exodus 34:6b-7** NIV

Since we are more than happy to embrace the generational blessings that come to us through our ancestors, we must also be willing to stand in identification for the curses that they have brought onto the family line. However, *blaming others for the curses in our life does not impress God.* We need to acknowledge that the sin is there and that we are part of the line that carries the curse and deal with it by forgiveness and repentance.

We must recognize that although we may not have personally introduced the sin in our family line we have authority as members of the family to bring the Cross to bear on the sin so that it is removed from our family line.

> *"Lord, the God of heaven, the great and awesome God, who keeps his covenant of love with those who love him and keep his commandments, let your ear be attentive and your eyes open to hear the prayer your servant is praying before you day and night for your servants, the people of Israel. I confess the*

94

sins we Israelites, including myself and my father's family, have committed against you. We have acted very wickedly toward you. We have not obeyed the commands, decrees and laws you gave your servant Moses." **Nehemiah 1:5-7** NIV

I prayed to the Lord my God and confessed: "Lord, the great and awesome God, who keeps his covenant of love with those who love him and keep his commandments, we have sinned and done wrong. We have been wicked and have rebelled; we have turned away from your commands and laws. We have not listened to your servants the prophets, who spoke in your name to our kings, our princes and our ancestors, and to all the people of the land...
All Israel has transgressed your law and turned away, refusing to obey you. "Therefore the curses and sworn judgments written in the Law of Moses, the servant of God, have been poured out on us, because we have sinned against you." **Daniel 9:3-6, 11** NIV

And you say, 'If we had lived in the days of our ancestors, we would not have taken part with them in shedding the blood of the prophets.' So you testify against yourselves that you are the descendants of those who murdered the prophets. Go ahead, then, and complete what your ancestors started!" **Matthew 23:30-32** NIV

PRAYER

LORD JESUS, I THANK you that you love me and that your desire is that I would have life and have it in abundance.

I DO HOWEVER CONFESS that I seem to lack that abundance in my life, as did also those in my ancestral line. I confess and agree with your word that all have sinned and fallen short of the glory of God.

I CONFESS THAT MY ancestors have sinned and that their sin still carries an impact to this very day.

I NOW, BY AN act of my will, choose to forgive and also repent on behalf of my ancestral line, for all the evil they have perpetrated and never repented of. I agree with your word that there are consequences for disobedience.

I NOW RENOUNCE THAT evil which has continued through the generational line. I lay it at the foot of the Lord Jesus Christ, and ask you, Lord, to remove it from my life and the life of my descendants.

I NOW APPROPRIATE YOUR forgiveness and the blessings available to me and my descendants through your work on the cross. AMEN.

The Influence Of Curses And Negative Words

There are many forms of curses that can operate in our lives. *Whenever a negative word, a curse, is spoken into us it will act like a poisonous dart that enters our soul and begins to rob us of joy and life.*

We often go through life not even considering the possibility that we may be operating under a curse.

Whatever way we have been cursed, we need to be aware that it has an impact on our life.

> *"The good man brings out of his good treasure what is good; and the evil man brings out of his evil treasure what is evil. But I tell you that every careless word that people speak, they shall give an accounting for it in the day of judgment. For by your words you will be justified, and by your words you will be condemned."* **Matthew 12:35-37**

The negative words that were spoken by our parents, when we were children, may still impact us today. The negative words spoken by some close relative, by a sibling, by teachers or even by school mates can still impact us today.

If the words that were lodged in our heart were not life giving and encouraging they may be the source of that which is robbing us of life today. Words impact us deeply since much of who we are is formed by words spoken to us. The words that still echo inside us keep us connected to the offender.

Negative words can easily become curses and we need to forgive those who spoke them. Then we can break the curse.

There can be a curse put in place by those who do not agree with the person's decision to become a Christian. It can come through family, friends, society, and culture.

> *Death and life are in the power of the tongue has the power of life and death, and those who love it will eat its fruit.* **Proverbs 18:2**

Negative words always carry with them the power to initiate a curse. This is particularly true what a woman conceives a child in sin or against her will; she may curse the child and wish it were gone from her womb. That is a death wish; and it affects the unborn child at a deep level.

It is always a good thing to pray and ask God if there are curses on our lives which are holding us, keeping us from being fully free. When Holy Spirit reminds us what those things may be, we need to remember that there is no condemnation in the Father's heart. However, the revelation is to bless and encourage us to take ownership of what Jesus died for.

PRAYER

FATHER GOD, I COME to you in the name of Jesus Christ of Nazareth, your only begotten son and my Lord and Savior.

JESUS, I THANK YOU that you became cursed for me.

LORD, I CHOOSE TO forgive those who have spoken a curse into my life, and I release them into the freedom of my forgiveness.

THROUGH YOUR NAME AND shed blood, I break the power of any curse spoken into my life, whether it was done carelessly or premeditated.

I ALSO ASK YOU to forgive me for any word, action, or thought that opened the door for a curse to begin operating in my life or the life of another person or place.

LORD, AS YOU FORGIVE me I also forgive each person who has been instrumental in bringing a curse into my life. I also forgive myself for participating in this action.

AS THESE CURSES ARE broken off my life, I now choose to appropriate the fullness of life that was gained on my behalf by my Lord and Savior, Jesus Christ, through his death on the cross on Calvary.

THANK YOU, LORD JESUS, for taking the curse from me and giving me freedom, fullness of life and hope for a productive and joyful future.

TEN

FAILURE TO RECOGNIZE AND RESIST THE ENEMY

It is not my belief that there is a demon under every rock or behind every bush; however, it is my belief that they are real and that they do operate in the world today. However we approach the problem of the demonic it must be done from a place of scriptural reality. The belief that Christians can't have demons may sound comforting; however, it does not match the reality or experience of our Christian walk today.

When our theology does not match the reality of the world we live in, we must re-examine our theology. If we do not believe that we have an enemy who is at work to bring harm to us at this very moment we will not acknowledge or resist him and we will be blindsided by his schemes.

> *But one whom you forgive anything, I forgive also; for indeed what I have forgiven, if I have forgiven anything, I did it for your sakes in the presence of Christ, so that no advantage would be taken of us by Satan, for we are not ignorant of his schemes.* **2Corinthians 2:10-11**

> *Put on the full armor of God, so that you will be able to stand firm against the schemes of the devil.* **Ephesians 6:11**

Faulty theology can block healing.

If a demon is holding the person in bondage, it will not be broken until the person agrees to have it dealt with.

The belief that says Christians can't have demons attached to them, working to undermine their Christian walk, is a demonic stronghold that needs to be confessed and renounced.

PRAYER

LORD, I REPENT FOR failing to believe your word that there is an enemy of my soul who wants to destroy me and those I love.

I REPENT FOR BELIEVING in the word of men when they declared that we cannot be attacked by the enemy or that we could not be oppressed and harassed. I believed their word when they said the enemy cannot even have a part in our lives.

I REPENT FOR GIVING the enemy free access to my life through not accepting that he is real and out to destroy your handiwork.

I RENOUNCE THE WORK of the enemy in my life and declare that under the guidance of Holy Spirit I will vigorously resist and cast out all and any part of his work in my life and the life of those I have spiritual authority over.

Not Resisting The Enemy

There are times when we must consciously fight the enemy and make every effort to resist the luring of temptation. Temptation is not a sin. It is an offering from the enemy who is looking for a place of vulnerability. When we succumb to temptation we allow the enemy to make inroads into our spiritual defenses. Our weakness is never an excuse for sin.

Be alert and sober mind. Your enemy the devil prowls around like a roaring lion looking for someone to devour.... **1 Peter 5:8** *NIV*

No temptation has overtaken you but such as is common to man; and God is faithful, who will not allow you to be tempted beyond what you are able, but with the temptation will provide the way of escape also, so that you will be able to endure it. **1 Corinthians 10:13**

Let no one say when he is tempted, "I am being tempted by God"; for God cannot be tempted by evil, and He Himself does not tempt anyone. **James 1:13**

Submit yourselves, then, to God. Resist the devil, and he will flee from you. Come near to God, and He will come near to you. **James 4:7-8** NIV

PRAYER

I ASK YOU, LORD, to forgive me for submitting to fear, doubt and insecurity and not resisting the enemy.

FORGIVE ME FOR NOT resisting the lies that were fed in to me: lies about you, Lord, lies about others and particularly lies about me.

I CONFESS AND REPENT for allowing fear to have a hold in my life. This thereby gave the enemy a foothold from which he could impact my actions and attitudes.

I CONFESS THAT I have allowed the enemy access to my emotions, particularly anger, and gave him free rein in parts of my life.

LORD, I CONFESS THAT *I have not submitted to you nor embraced your truth. Therefore, I have not been able to resist the onslaught of the enemy.*

LORD, I NOW CHOSE *to submit to you and your leading. I choose to stand my ground in you in the battle for my soul.*

THANK YOU, LORD JESUS, *that you are my friend, my ally in this battle, and that with you I have nothing to fear*

ELEVEN

FAILURE TO FACE REALITY

The tendency to want to avoid truth is a major problem many of us face today. We prefer the illusion of stability to the stark reality that something may be wrong or even that we are wrong. We often choose to see things in a way that is to our advantage and therefore get caught in a trap that will keep us from moving into the wholeness God wants us to appropriate.

Denial

Denial is a contradiction of the facts, where a person refuses to accept the reality, declaring that the evidence is not the truth.

There are many who walk in contradiction to reality. Declaring that something isn't so does not change their reality or circumstance. Yet, there are those who refuse to accept that they are ill or in need of help or deliverance because they do not believe that as a Christian any of this could happen to them. Therefore they deny that they may be hurt, angry, disappointed, or even suffering. Believing that they are walking in faith, they fail to see that they are in denial. Their standards are not from God, but often they are learned beliefs either from their families or the religious institutions they are a part of.

God deals in reality! Healing is available, but we must appropriate it.

We need to deal with this ungodly pattern and it may require teaching and releasing those we minister to from ungodly beliefs or teachings that deny reality. This type of teaching has the appearance of holiness, but in reality it is a subtle trap. The person believes he is "standing in faith," even quoting positive Bible verses about his freedom and healing. At the same time, he is denying the facts of his condition, thereby blocking other areas where the Lord is seeking to touch him.

In fact this attitude of "faith" can hinder the Lord's hand from moving in their lives. This does not deny the fact that we must walk by faith, but we can only do so when we acknowledge the situation and ask God to see us through the circumstances we find ourselves in. Scripture is clear; we do not deny the circumstance, but we thank God in the circumstance.

> *Rejoice always;*
> *pray continually,*
> *give thanks in all circumstances; for this is*
> *God's will for you in Christ Jesus.*
> **1 Thessalonians 5:16-18**

PRAYER

I CONFESS AND REPENT for failing to accept the reality of the situation that I am in. I have presumed that you will honor unreality and bless me while I walk in denial.

I CONFESS THAT I have used denial to avoid facing the truth, and that I have used your word to avoid facing the truth of what is really going on around me.

LORD, I ASK YOU to teach me what is truth and what is wishful thinking.

I CONFESS THAT BY standing on certain scriptures I have failed to act on the truth available to me.

I HAVE WAITED FOR your hand of provision while you were opening a door of opportunity.

I CONFESS THAT I failed to act in ways that were life giving to me or others because I refused to move from my ungodly attitudes or beliefs.

I REPENT FOR NOT heeding the words of your servants, failing to appropriate the truth of your counselors; I chose to go my own way.

I ASK YOU, LORD, to forgive me for the times in which I thought I was being a good witness.

I CONFESS I WAS only trying to impress or condemn others through my actions.

LORD, FORGIVE ME FOR refusing to see the truth and for walking in denial. Help me be a person of truth and reality.

Lack Of Honesty And Transparency

When our "name" becomes more important than acknowledging our needs or failings, we create a blockage. The wall of mistrust blocks the free flow of God's healing. Our fear of being honest and vulnerable gives the enemy an easy way to keep us locked up in our pain.

> *Pride goes before destruction, a haughty spirit before a fall.* **Proverbs 16:18** NIV

> *Therefore confess your sins to each other and pray for each other so that you may be healed. The prayer of a righteous person is powerful and effective.* **James 5:16** NIV

PRAYER

LORD, I CONFESS MY fear and lack of trust in those who walk with me in the brotherhood of the saints.

I CONFESS THAT I have been afraid, and therefore have not been honest or open. I have withheld part of me, not allowing others to see me as I truly am.

I REPENT FOR MY fear and renounce the control it caused me to live under.

LORD, I NOW ASK you to forgive me for my lack of honesty and my fear of transparency.

I CHOOSE TO BEGIN to be more real and honest in my dealings with those you place in my life.

Not Wanting To Be Healed

There are those people who will go to various places looking for healing, but the very process of having prayer and being the center of focused attention is the thing they crave. They want their illness; it becomes the vehicle that gives them what they long for—the prayers and sympathy from those around them—and it can easily become part of their identity. They enjoy their illness. It gets them a sense of being important and receiving the care they hunger after.

Their fear is that once they are healed, the care they received will be lost. Without the illness, they may not be able to hold people's attention or affection. This may be something they do consciously, but often they are not even aware they are doing it. Sometimes their need for attention overrides their desire for healing.

The individual must <u>want</u> to be healed. When the disease gives them identity, they are missing the very essence of the Father's love: to set the captive free. When the things that hold us in bondage give us identity, we are most certainly moving in a spirit of poverty and slavery.

PRAYER

LORD, I CONFESS AND repent for having used my illness, my sickness and my infirmity as a way of getting attention. It has become my identity.

I HAVE USED IT as a crutch and a means of getting pity and time from others. I have used my condition as a way of manipulating those around me. It is sin and I repent of it now.

I CONFESS THAT I have had people pray for me, but secretly what I wanted was their attention more than the healing you have for me.

FORGIVE ME, LORD, FOR using my illness to get what you have always had for me: a purpose, a destiny and an identity in you.

THANK YOU LORD THAT as you forgive me, you will release the healing I truly need into every part of my being.

Unresolved Guilt

Real or imagined guilt can easily block healing.

> *I acknowledged my sin to You, And my iniquity I did not hide; I said, "I will confess my transgressions to the LORD"; And You forgave the guilt of my sin. Selah.*
> **Psalms 32:5**

> *"Therefore, there is now no condemnation for those who are in Christ Jesus, because through Christ Jesus the law of the Spirit of life set me free from the law of sin and death." * **Romans 8:1** NIV

The guilt we carry can cause us to believe that we don't deserve God's mercy or his gift of healing in our lives. We may stay in self condemnation for something which God has already forgiven us. The guilt is easily empowered when we refuse to believe that God's forgiveness is sufficient to deal with our sin.

Still others believe that the pain, stress or disease is from God and should therefore be embraced as a form of sanctification or even punishment for past failures. This belief ultimately tries to add to what Jesus did on the cross. It attempts to earn through self-denial and punishment the grace and love of God that is so freely available.

Part of the problem may be our inability to accept and walk in God's forgiveness and love. It often seems easier to carry the guilt, than to believe that in spite of our failures we are still loved and accepted by a perfect God.

> *Jesus replied "I tell you the truth, everyone who sins is a slave to sin. Now a slave has no permanent place in the family, but a son belongs to it forever. So if the Son sets you free, you will be free indeed."* **John 8:34-36** *NIV*

The demonic, having tempted us into sin, will now try to hold us in guilt. If we embrace the guilt, it will then lock us into a place where we can't believe that we are forgiven, or where we can't forgive ourselves. Now we not only need to deal with the sin, but also with the guilt.

> *Or do you think lightly of the riches of His kindness and tolerance and patience, not knowing that the kindness of God leads you to repentance?* **Romans 2:4**

Once we have repented, (which is a gift from God), and been forgiven, we have to appropriate the full mercy of God—not only His forgiveness, but also His cleansing and acceptance.

> *"If we confess our sins, he is faithful and just and will forgive us our sins and purify us from all unrighteousness."* **1 John 1:9** NIV

There may even be a belief that the guilt is from God. He may have forgiven us, but we believe that we still need to be punished for the sin—holding on to the guilt seems to be the best way of doing that.

> *There is no fear in love; but perfect love casts out fear, because fear involves punishment, and the one who fears is not perfected in love. We love, because He first loved us.*
> **1 John 4:18-19**

> *Therefore there is now no condemnation for those who are in Christ Jesus. For the law of the Spirit of life in Christ Jesus has set you free from the law of sin and of death.*
> **Romans 8:1-2**

If we do not believe the word of God, then fear and condemnation will release a spirit of guilt that can and will torment us. Once fear and guilt take root, we may get into the cycle of believing that we have not been forgiven, confessing the same sin again and again trying to remove the guilt.

We may get to the point of believing that if we only could say the right prayer (the formula prayer), in just the right way, then

God will release us from the guilt. We are now into "works" and will continually fall short of the mark. The enemy will make sure of it, because none of this is from God. The enemy has us in a trap: forgiven, but not free from the self-condemnation.

When we believe with our feelings, we are opening ourselves to potential trouble. We should not ignore our feelings, <u>unless</u> they tell us something that is contrary to the word of God.

> *If we are faithless, He remains faithful, for He cannot deny Himself.* **2 Timothy 2:13**

> *All Scripture is inspired by God and profitable for teaching, for reproof, for correction, for training in righteousness; so that the man of God may be adequate, equipped for every good work.* **2 Timothy 3:16-17**

> *So Jesus was saying to those Jews who had believed Him, "If you continue in My word, then you are truly disciples of Mine;*
> *...and you will know the truth, and the truth will make you free."* **John 8:31, 36**

As Jesus preaches about the freedom that he brings into the lives of those who obey him, he is declaring more than just freedom. He is declaring that we also belong in the Father's house.

> *"So I say to you: Ask and it will be given to you; seek and you will find; knock and the door will be opened to you.*

For everyone who asks, receives; and he who seeks, finds; and to him who knocks, it will be opened.

...If you then, being evil, know how to give good gifts to your children, how much more will your heavenly Father give the Holy Spirit to those who ask Him?" **Luke 11:9, 13**

Jesus is again declaring the goodness of the Father. He prefaces the story with a promise—that those who ask will receive. This is not the way we are used to receiving, but it comes from a heavenly Father's point of view!

"So I say to you: Ask and it will be given to you; seek and you will find; knock and the door will be opened to you." **Luke 11:9** NIV

When we ask for God's forgiveness, it will be an unconditional gift, with freedom and acceptance. As the word of God says, when Jesus set us free we were definitely set free. This freedom has with it also a release of the guilt that would want to keep us in bondage.

"So if the Son makes you free, you will be free indeed. **John 8:36**

PRAYER

LORD, I CONFESS THAT I have allowed guilt to control my life and failed to appropriate your love and forgiveness.

I HAVE FAILED TO believe your word that says that there is now no condemnation for me since you have rescued me and paid the price for my sin.

I HAVE FAILED TO believe that you have taken the punishment for my weakness and set me on solid ground.

LORD, I REPENT FOR allowing the guilt to define who I am, and for denying the truth of your word. I am set free through Jesus Christ and His work on the cross.

I RENOUNCE GUILT and choose to walk in the grace of being forgiven, cleansed and having my debt paid.

I THANK YOU AND bless you, Lord, for setting me free of condemnation and the prison of self imposed guilt.

Twelve

Hopelessness

When we become hopeless, we embrace a level of desperation; we lose the expectation of being able to recover or attaining any kind of relief in the future. We begin to settle for the inevitable end. Waiting for the end, losing hope, is a dangerous thing; it keeps us from pressing in to the promises of God for our lives, the lives of others or even the lives of our communities. Once we come to a place of hopelessness we cease to be life givers or even to expect life from others.

Negative Thoughts And Attitudes

When we are hopeless we develop a tendency to be judgmental and negative about most situations we face. We are prone to expect the worst. *Those things that are not life-giving can cause us to remain in a place of bondage and limitations.*

We live in a society that lives in an atmosphere of mistrust. We have carried that mindset over into almost everything we do, even to our relationship with God. It is a major block to blessing and healing.

Our thoughts will generate life around us; whether it is good or bad is often up to us. The scripture is clear; our attitude and outlook have to be positive, or else we will slip into the place of hopelessness.

Rejoice always.
Pray continually,
give thanks in all circumstances, for this is
God's will for you in Christ Jesus.
Do not quench the Spirit.
Do not treat prophecies with contempt but
test them all; hold on to what is good, reject
every kind of evil.

May God himself, the God of peace, sanctify
you through and through. May your whole
spirit, soul and body be kept blameless at the
coming of our Lord Jesus Christ.
1 Thessalonians 5:16-23 *NIV*

As we ask the Father to reveal the blocks in our lives, those things that give the enemy a right to keep us in bondage, we are taking more and more responsibility for the wholeness in our lives. As we remove the hindrances to the Father's healing love, we begin to move into a place of maturity as sons of the living God.

PRAYER

LORD, I CONFESS AND repent for all the ways
that I have entertained and delighted in my negative
thoughts about others.

I RECOGNIZE THAT HAS shaped my attitude towards them in a way that is not honoring to you or to them.

I CONFESS AND REPENT that I have even extended that to you, Lord.

I ALSO CONFESS AND repent for the negative ways I have thought about myself and how this has shaped my attitudes toward myself and the world.

LORD, I CONFESS THIS as sin and I ask you to forgive me and cleanse me of this defiling way of thinking.

I AGREE THAT THIS is a breeding ground for the enemy to operate in my life.

I REPENT OF THIS and I ask you to help me renew my mind so that it is conformed to the image and nature of Jesus Christ.

Looking To Man Rather Than God

There are many times when our faith is in the one who may have the "gift of healing," rather than in the giver of the gift.

We need to be cautious that we do not look at the person doing the praying as the source of the healing. This is a trap and can be harmful to both parties if this is allowed to happen. We can easily lose sight of the true healer and take our focus off God and place it on man. When we look at people and see them as the solution to our problem we are in danger of putting them in the place that only belongs to God. As a result, we may come to someone and put our faith in that person to pray for us to be healed through their anointing.

The idolatry of "the anointing" is prevalent in many parts of the church today. God, in his love, will not allow it; he will not allow it either for the sake of his servant who is ministering, or for the one who comes seeking a touch.

This is what the Lord says:
"Cursed is the one who trusts in man, who draws strength from mere flesh and whose heart turns away from the Lord.
But blessed is the one who trusts in the Lord, whose confidence is in him." **Jeremiah 17:5, 7** *NIV*

PRAYER

LORD JESUS, I ASK you to forgive me for failing to turn to you when there was a need in my life or the life of someone I loved.

I CONFESS AND REPENT for having turned to man rather than you as my first recourse.

I ASK YOU TO forgive me for my unbelief and for trusting man more than you.

I CONFESS AND REPENT for believing more in the wisdom of man than the wisdom of God.

I CONFESS AND REPENT for not trusting that you would or could help in this situation.

I THANK YOU FOR the wisdom you gave man to be able to extract medicine from the things that you have given the world.

LORD, I ACKNOWLEDGE THAT without you there is no life, and that you are the source of all life.

Trusting Something Other Than God

When we look at people for our source of hope, we will inevitably be disappointed. When we are overwhelmed with disappointment it is easy to give up hope and move into despair.

We are never to give up hope. Our hope is in Christ and He will never fail us. Do we trust Him enough to submit ourselves fully to him?

...and hope does not disappoint, because the love of God has been poured out within our hearts through the Holy Spirit who was given to us. For while we were still helpless, at the right time Christ died for the ungodly. **Romans 5:5-6**

We want each of you to show this same diligence to the very end, so that what you hope for may be fully realized. **Hebrews 6:11** *NIV*

PRAYER

LORD JESUS, I CONFESS and repent for not believing your promise never to leave or forsake me, now, tomorrow or ever.

I CONFESS AND I repent that I have looked at my circumstances and declared that they are beyond hope, Lord.

I CONFESS AND I repent that I have embraced hopelessness, and therefore have brought lifelessness into my spirit.

I ALSO CONFESS AND I repent that I have placed my hope in things, men and finances-- those things you declare to be hopeless.

I CONFESS AND REPENT for having more trust in men than in your ability to save me.

LORD JESUS, I NOW renounce my hope and trust in the things of the world and choose to trust and hope in you only.

YOU ARE THE ONLY one who never changes and therefore, are fully trustworthy and the source of all hope.

Thirteen

Carelessness

Where hopelessness has its greatest impact on how we feel and respond to the world and those around us, carelessness will undermine the confidence of others in us and our ability to be responsible. It is seen as a lack of concern or a lack of maturity. We create a major stumbling block in our lives when we are careless about the things of God.

We are responsible to maintain a healthy life style; this includes how we nourish our spirit, our soul and our bodies. We are also responsible to look after, to steward, that which has been entrusted to us. Whether it is some one else's life (spouse, children, students, or employees), property or finances, we are still responsible.

We are accountable when we neglect to take care of the things God has entrusted to us. We need to address these issues before expecting to receive God's best for us.

This does not mean that God won't heal. It means only that we need to do our part in having a clean vessel to receive the healing from His hands.

What agreement is there between the temple of God and idols? For you are the temple of the living God. As God has said, "I will live

with them and walk among them, and I will
be their God, and they will be my people."

2 Corinthians 6:16 NIV

PRAYER

LORD JESUS, I CONFESS and repent for the
ways I have neglected to honor you, by being
irresponsible for myself, the people and the things
of the kingdom you have entrusted to me.

I REPENT FOR THE negligent and self-serving
way that I have approached and discharged the
tasks you have given me to fulfill.

I CONFESS AND REPENT that through
my negligence others have suffered and that
even their suffering did not change the way I
do things.

I SPECIFICALLY REPENT FOR the way I
have neglected my own physical body and through
that neglect have opened myself to sickness and
disease.

TEACH ME LORD TO walk in wholeness,
not only of spirit and soul, but also in my
body.

Expecting God To Heal Us On Our Own Terms

When we have not been taught to be responsible or worse still, have been spoiled in our upbringing, we may believe that life centers on us and comes to us on our terms.

> God is God and we are not. He will do it in His time and in His way.

We cannot come to God and demand that He give us what we want on our terms. When we have already predetermined how that is to take place, we are essentially dictating our terms to God.

> *Do not be deceived, God is not mocked; for whatever a man sows, this he will also reap. For the one who sows to his own flesh will from the flesh reap corruption, but the one who sows to the Spirit will from the Spirit reap eternal life. Let us not lose heart in doing good, for in due time we will reap if we do not grow weary.* **Galatians 6:7-9**

> *Praise the LORD! Praise the LORD, O my soul! I will praise the LORD while I live; I will sing praises to my God while I have my being. Do not trust in princes, In mortal man, in whom there is no salvation.* **Psalms 146:1-3**

God is God and we are not. He will do it in His time and in His way.

The story of Naaman is a wonderful example of God's sovereignty. God first deals with a powerful man's pride and then releases his healing.

> *And Naaman came with his horses and with his chariot, and stood at the door of the house of Elisha.*
> *And Elisha sent a messenger to him, saying, Go and wash in Jordan seven times, and your flesh shall come to you, and you shall be clean.*
> *But Naaman was angry, and went away...*
> *And his servants came near and spoke to him and said, My father, if the prophet had told you to do a great thing, would you not have done it? How much rather then, when he says to you, Wash and be clean?*
> *And he went down and dipped seven times in Jordan, according to the saying of the man of God. And his flesh came again like the flesh of a little boy, and he was clean. And he returned to the man of God, he and all his company. And he came and stood before him. And he said, Behold, now I know that there is no God in all the earth, but in Israel. And now please take a blessing from your servant.*
> **2 Kings 5:9-11, 13-15**

To trust that God will do things His way is not always the easiest thing for us. However, we must trust His sovereignty in all circumstances as we begin to walk in true sonship.

PRAYER

DEAR LORD JESUS, I repent for presuming to tell you how to answer my prayer.

I HAVE PRESUMED THAT I could tell you how to do that which I request by telling you how, when and why you should do this thing for me.

I HAVE RELIED UPON my own understanding and failed to trust you with my needs.

LORD, I TAKE MY hand and my control off this situation. I trust it to you; knowing that only what is good comes from you.

THANK YOU FOR FORGIVING me and cleansing me from my presumption.

Improper Care Of The Body

Our physical body is the temple of the Holy Spirit. As such we need to take care of our body: to honor it, to nurture it and minister life-giving activities to it.

Good health is something we need to strive for without allowing it to become the primary focus of our lives.

*Don't you not know that you yourselves are
God's temple and that God's Spirit dwells in
your midst?, If anyone destroys God's temple,
God will destroy that person; for God's
temple is sacred, and you together are that
temple.* **1 Corinthians 3:16-17** NIV

*It is God's will that you should be sanctified:,
that you should avoid sexual immorality; that
each of you should learn to control your own
body in a way that is holy and honorable, not
in passionate lust live the pagans, who do not
know God;* **1 Thessalonians 4:3-5** NIV

PRAYER

*FATHER, YOUR WORD SAYS that you knit
me together in my mother's womb, and that I am
fearfully and wonderfully made.*

*YOUR WORD SAYS THAT my body is the
temple of your Holy Spirit that you have
chosen to abide in me.*

*I CONFESS THAT I have not honored your
temple or kept it holy for your purposes.*

*I ASK YOU TO forgive me for abusing my body
through neglect, through abuse and through cursing it.*

*I CONFESS THAT I have used your temple
for my own purposes and gratification. I
confess that I have gratified the desires of*

my flesh rather than the desire of my spirit.

I CONFESS THAT I have either hated my body or worshiped my body and in the process ignored your purposes for this, your temple.

I CONFESS THIS AS sin and I repent of doing this. I ask you now to sanctify your temple and again take priority in my flesh.

I DO THIS IN the name of my Lord and Savior, your Son, Jesus Christ.

Fourteen

God's Sovereignty

Sometimes one of the hardest things for us to come to terms with is that God truly is sovereign and that he is not answerable to us. We often presume that since he created us, loves us, knows all there is to know about us, and was willing to let Jesus die for us, that this somehow makes him accountable to us—that we can tell him how he should do things for us and for others. We often find ourselves getting to the place where we even proclaim the unfairness of God for not making things happen the way we want or expect them to.

God's Timing

> *There is a time for everything, and a season for every activity under the heavens;*
> *a time to be born and a time to die; a time to plant, and a time to uproot, a time to kill and a time to heal, a time to tear down and a time to build,* **Ecclesiastes 3:1-3** NIV

There are times when God moves in power and healing occurs immediately. There are other times when God may want to accomplish other things in our lives. He will use the present circumstance to teach us a truth that is very important for us to learn before He heals us.

"For My thoughts are not your thoughts, neither are your ways My ways," declares the LORD.

"As the heavens are higher than the earth, so are my ways higher than your ways and my thoughts than your thoughts. As the rain and the snow come down from heaven, and do not return to it without watering the earth and making it bud and flourish, so that it yields seed for the sower and bread for the eater, so is my word that goes out from my mouth; it will not return to me empty, but it will accomplish what I desire and achieve the purpose for which I sent it." **Isaiah 55:6-11** *NIV*

As we prayerfully wait for God to move, we must be attentive to whatever else he may be doing while we continue to pray. It is quite amazing how quickly people lose faith in God when the thing they prayed for is not accomplished. There is a time when we must be unrelenting in prayer and not tire from asking for God's blessing and healing.

> **As we mature, we begin to rest, and trust more in the sovereign actions of God.**

Persevering is more than hanging on in prayer; it is coming to a place of rest even in our need. It is a place where the relationship is more important than the healing. It is the place where we can come to rest in the knowledge and assurance that God is never late the way we understand being late.

In prayer, we need to trust God's timing. What often happens is that we determine the length of time it should take for the healing to take place. When we become impatient, frustrated, or even angry at God, we are presuming in our relationship with him.

There is a conflict between God's timing and our timing. In the conflict however, God begins to reveal our heart.

> *The Lord is not slow about His promise, as some count slowness, but is patient toward you, not wishing for any to perish but for all to come to repentance.* **2Peter 3:9**

Part of growing in faith is the ability to wait on the Lord.

> *Yet those who wait for the LORD Will gain new strength; They will mount up with wings like eagles, They will run and not get tired, They will walk and not become weary.* **Isaiah 40:31**

As we mature, we begin to rest, and trust more in the sovereign actions of God.

PRAYER

DEAR LORD JESUS, I confess that I have presumed to know your will and therefore your timing.

I REPENT FOR BEING angry with you and for even doubting your will to heal.

I DECLARE THAT YOUR ways are better and that I do not understand the plans that you have for me or those I love and care for.

LORD, I ASK YOU to forgive my presumption and I do declare it as sin.

I RENOUNCE NOW THE belief that I know what you should do and that when you don't do it my way I have a right to be angry at you.

THANK YOU, LORD, THAT you forgive and that you cleanse me of my sin and my unrighteousness.

Sickness Unto Death

"When he heard this, Jesus said, 'This sickness will not end in death. No, it is for God's glory so that God's Son may be glorified through it." **John 11:4** NIV

Some sickness is unto death; there is a time when God wants to take people home. We may even have to pray that the Lord release the person into eternal life, rather than trying to pray for their healing.

We need to seek God on how and when to pray this type of prayer. However, *we still need to pray no matter what the person's age.*

PRAYER

LORD, I CONFESS MY dismay and anger at you for not doing things my way, and in my time frame.

I CONFESS THAT I did not ask you for your timing.

I CONFESS THAT MY need and desire for the one I loved was greater than my trust in you.

LORD, WHERE I HELD on beyond what you wanted me to hold on, I repent.

LORD, WHERE I RELEASED before it was time to release, I repent.

LORD JESUS, TEACH ME your perfect timing in all things, so that I may release all things into your care. I want to be in unity with you in all I do.

Sickness is still an enemy that must be overcome. Recently there has been more and more revelation from the Lord on how to pray and deal with the roots of many of the physical problems our world is facing today. We need to continue to pray for more and more revelation in this whole area of ministry.

Fifteen

Anti-Semitism

Anti-Semitism is a part of our society and the world's attitude towards God's chosen people, the Jews. There does not seem to be a time when the prejudice, persecution and the attempt to eliminate this people has not been part of their history. Today it is rampant not just in the Middle East. Almost anywhere in the world we will find the separation between the Jewish people and those who are not part of their bloodline. The scripture is clear about God's commitment to the descendants of Abraham, Isaac and Jacob,

> *Now the LORD said to Abram, "Go forth from your country, And from your relatives And from your father's house, To the land which I will show you; And I will make you a great nation, And I will bless you, And make your name great; And so you shall be a blessing; And I will bless those who bless you, And the one who curses you I will curse. And in you all the families of the earth will be blessed."* **Genesis 12:1-3**

The constant persecution and attempts at extermination are prime examples of how the enemy will use prejudice and fear to attempt to destroy those God calls his own.

> *"Therefore, say to the Israelites: 'I am the Lord, and I will bring you out from under the yoke of the Egyptians. I will free you from*

*being slaves to them, and I will redeem you
with an outstretched arm and with mighty
acts of judgment. I will take you as my own
people, and I will be your God"* **Exodus
6:6-7**

Prejudices will always lead to separation and cursing.
When our attitude towards God's chosen people is
one of bigotry, we are cursing the ones He loves and
calling upon ourselves the curses of God. Those who
are under God's curse will not benefit from his
blessings. Therefore they will not walk in the fullness
of healing and freedom.

PRAYER

*LORD, I CONFESS AND repent for the sins of
my ancestors who failed to bless those you blessed.
Instead, they cursed them by their attitudes, words
and actions.*

*LORD, I ALSO CONFESS and repent for my
attitudes, words and actions towards those you call
your people.*

*LORD, I REPENT FOR the times I remained
silent and failed to speak up and declare your
truth about those you call your own. I am as much
to blame as my ancestors and therefore walk
under the same pronouncement they did.*

LORD, I NOW ASK you to forgive my ancestors for their sin and break the power of the curse over my life and the life of my descendants.

THROUGH YOUR SHED BLOOD and the work of the cross, I declare that I am grafted in to the line of Abraham, Isaac and Jacob.

AND I NOW CHOOSE to bless those you bless in Jesus' name. Amen

Sixteen

End Thoughts

For I am confident of this very thing, that He who began a good work in you will perfect it until the day of Christ Jesus.
Philippians 1:6

God is always at work in us, for us and with us, illuminating that which he wants us to address in our lives. He is revealing those things that block us from both intimacy and the healing he wants us to experience.

The blockages are always a hindrance. Dealing with them does not force God to act on our behalf, but it does clear the way for him to do so.

The preceding chapters present only a very small overview of what can keep us from receiving all the good that God has for us. Having said that, however, God is not limited by our limitations; he can, and often does in his sovereignty, intervene on our behalf.

> *Let the wicked forsake their ways and the unrighteous their thoughts.*
> *Let them turn to the Lord, and he will have mercy on them, and to our God, for he will freely pardon.* **Isaiah 55:7**

We do not want to imply in any way that if we deal with those things, which are contrary to God's will, that He is then obligated to bring healing into our lives. *Healing is one of God's gifts to us, and therefore cannot be earned.* We don't have a right to demand this gift from him. We can, however, position ourselves to receive those things that will bring release into our lives.

> *"If I shut up the heavens so that there is no rain, or if I command the locust to devour the land, or if I send pestilence among My people, and My people who are called by My name humble themselves and pray and seek My face and turn from their wicked ways, then I will hear from heaven, will forgive their sin and will heal their land. Now My eyes will be open and My ears attentive to the prayer offered in this place.* " **2 Chronicles 7:13-15**

One of the problems, or traps, in dealing with a subject like this, is that we begin to focus on the issues. We also focus on the blockages for the sake of getting healed, rather than deal with the bigger issue of hindrances to our relationship with Him.

> *"...for your heavenly Father knows that you need all these things." "But seek first His kingdom and His righteousness, and all these things will be added to you."* **Matthew 6:32-33**

In our desire to be healed, we seek the healing apart from the things of the kingdom and a deeper relationship with the Lord. Ultimately we end up trying to use God for our own benefit at the exclusion of a deeper level of intimacy.

We are often like a child who comes to its parent seeking the resources for the things it wants. The child is doing and being what it believes the parents want, so that it can obtain its desired object. It is *doing* for the parent rather than building on the affection of the parents.

Simply stated, we use mom and dad to get what we want. God will not be used as a means to an end. He is after all, the start of all things and the end of all things.

Healing is one of God's gifts to us and therefore cannot be earned.

"I am the Alpha and the Omega," says the Lord God, "who is and who was and who is to come, the Almighty." **Revelations 1:8**

Made in the USA
Columbia, SC
14 March 2018